Mastering Old Testament Facts

PROGRAMMED READING

ART AND ACTIVITIES

TESTS

to get it all down PAT

BOOK 4
Prophetic Writings

Madeline H. Beck
Lamar Williamson, Jr.

Sketches
EVA STIMSON

John Knox Press
ATLANTA

International Standard Book Number: 0-8042-0137-4
© John Knox Press 1981
Printed in the United States of America

The Old Testament

The book you are about to read is Sacred Scripture for three of the world's great religions. It is the Scripture for Judaism. Islam, while giving highest authority to the Koran, still understands Israel's Scripture to be inspired and holy. Christians call these books the "Old Testament." They comprise about three-fourths of the Christian Bible, while writings of the early church, called the "New Testament," make up one-fourth. When the New Testament writers speak of the "Scripture," it is almost always to the Old Testament that they refer.

Men and women of all three faiths, as well as those of other faiths and those of no faith, continue to find the books of the Old Testament appealing, nourishing, beautiful, and stimulating -- as well as annoying, boring, and difficult. Many believe that these writings come from God; all agree that they belong to all humankind. None who care about humanity or literature or God should try to live in ignorance of their content.

This Book

Mastering Old Testament Facts is a guide for individuals or groups who want to know the basic content of the Old Testament. While it has been designed for individual use, it can easily be adapted for use by study groups or classes.

Like its companion, *Mastering New Testament Facts,* it can be used in local churches and military chapels, as a course supplement in schools and colleges, by candidates preparing for ordination exams, by potential church officers or teachers, and by individuals at home.

Purpose and Stance

The purpose of *Mastering Old Testament Facts* is in one way very modest. It focuses on a limited selection of basic content items: outline and sequence, persons, places, events, and characteristic features. Historical, literary and theological questions are set aside or receive only minimal attention.

In another sense, however, the purpose of this book is quite ambitious. The user should achieve 90 percent mastery of the material taught, or 70 percent growth above low pre-test scores.

By "facts" the authors intend no historical judgment. In line with its purpose, this guide aims at neutrality on debated historical and theological issues. Though it is impossible to read or to ask questions about a text without some interpretation, the authors have made a conscious effort to reduce interpretive elements to a minimum and to leave users maximum room for discussion and private judgment.

The authors are well aware that the Old Testament was designed to do far more than transmit information. They hope that this survey of content will lead readers to pursue the deeper intentions of the material either in groups that use this guide or in other appropriate contexts. Users should be warned that even if they score 100 percent on all tests, it will not mean that they have mastered the Bible!

Suggestions for Individual Study

1. Read and follow carefully each set of instructions, beginning with "Before You Use This Book," page 1.

2. Plan for sufficie. t time at each sitting to finish a logical block of biblical material, but not so long as to get bored or tired (30 minutes to 2 hours).

3. The *Good News Bible* (Today's English Version) is the most helpful translation to use with *Mastering Old Testament Facts*. However, other versions of the Old Testament may be used if differences in wording do not upset you.

4. Given the limited purpose of this book, you may wish to supplement it with a good commentary, Bible dictionary, and atlas.

Suggestions for Group Study

1. Each participant should have a copy of *Mastering Old Testament Facts* and the *Good News Bible*.

2. The leader should help participants with instructions in the book that might not be clear to some.

3. The group should balance time for discussion with time for individual study. Either covenant to spend an agreed time in individual study outside class, or use alternate meeting periods for individual study and for group discussion, or use half of each class period for individual work and the remaining half for discussion.

4. During individual study each participant should note one or two points most urgently needing group attention.

5. Someone should be responsible to look for other resources when group discussion does not resolve difficulties.

6. The leader should be sure all members have opportunities to participate, and that there is both freedom and direction in the discussion.

ACKNOWLEDGMENTS

Mr. and Mrs. Robert Hallock of Miami provided working space and substantial assistance during the writing of Books Two, Three, and Four.

Students at the Presbyterian School of Christian Education tried out the material, caught errors, and offered valuable suggestions. Dr. Malcolm C. McIver, Jr., professor of Christian Education, worked closely with the authors in scheduling and guiding use of the manuscripts as well as collating student comments.

To all of them the authors express their hearty thanks.

CONTENTS

BEFORE YOU USE THIS BOOK...

This study guide to the Old Testament appears in four books and has been designed to help you learn the content and structure of the Old Testament in the shortest possible time.

The books are: 1. *Introduction and Pentateuch*
2. *Historical Books*
3. *Poetry and Wisdom*
4. *Prophetic Writings*

Description

All four books use the PAT system (<u>P</u>rogrammed reading, <u>A</u>rt and activities, and <u>T</u>ests), which enables the student to get the facts down "pat." The approach followed is one which uses learning methods successfully employed both in public school education and in industry, but adapted to the biblical material. *Mastering Old Testament Facts* incorporates some aspects of programmed instruction and some aspects of a workbook. All of the techniques used in this study--pre-tests, guided reading, drawings, charts, section and unit tests--are ways of preparing or reinforcing one's memory. The goal is 90 percent mastery of the items selected for retention, or 70 percent growth.

Learning Process

Mastery of this material proceeds through five stages--one diagnostic, and four learning and evaluative.

1. Pre-test

The first, diagnostic stage is the pre-test you will take before you begin each unit. It will measure your present mastery of the Bible content taught in that unit and will acquaint you with the types of questions you will be expected to answer. It is not an evaluation, but a way of learning, so don't be disturbed if you do not know the material. If you already know it, you do not need to study it. On the other hand, the lower your pre-test score, the more gratifying may be your growth as measured by the final (unit) test.

2. Guided Reading

As you begin to learn, you will be asked to read the Bible itself a few chapters at a time. *Mastering Old Testament Facts* will guide you as you read by numbered outline headings which call attention to the structure of the biblical book and by questions which invite you to notice certain items in the passage. Guided reading pages are divided into three or four parts, each of which is called a "frame." You will not read straight down the page, but you will work through all the top frames of one unit before returning to begin working through the second frames on each page.

Used properly, both the numbers and the capitalization of the frame headings will help you remember the biblical book's outline. The first digit refers to the section of the unit. The second and third digits refer to major divisions in the book, while capital letters at the end of a heading number refer to subdivisions. Do not be surprised if outline numbers jump from 15 to 20, for instance, as you move from Part One of Isaiah to Part Two! Major divisions are written in ALL CAPITAL LETTERS and subheadings are Initially Capitalized.

Drawings on question pages are used to reinforce your learning of the book's structure. Drawings on answer pages will reinforce one or two of the items taught in each frame.

3. Section Tests

At the end of each biblical book, or on completion of an entire series of frames, you will be tested on items emphasized in the guided reading. You may refresh your memory of the structure, major themes, and key quotations by studying the chart provided for each book just before you take the section test. Due to the large amount of significant items in some of the books (like Isaiah and Jeremiah), section tests will not always include every item to which your attention has been drawn. However, they will include every item you are expected to retain, organized into categories which will help you to know what you are learning and to measure your progress in each area. If you score less than 90 percent on any part of the section test, you should review the relevant material in the study guide and in the Old Testament.

4. Unit Test

When you have completed all sections at the 90 percent level, a final test will evaluate your mastery of the biblical books in each unit. By using the scoring charts and growth record at the back of the study guide you can easily determine your growth in knowledge of biblical content.

5. Study References

Scripture references are given for all unit test answers. By checking the references for any items you miss on a unit test, you can complete your mastery of that unit's content. If you score less than 90 percent you should review any areas of weakness before proceeding to another unit. This does not apply if your growth from the score you made on the pre-test was more than 70 percent.

PENTATEUCH
HISTORICAL BOOKS
POETRY AND WISDOM
PROPHETIC WRITINGS

The fourth and last great division of the Old Testament, the Prophetic Writings, is called the "Latter Prophets" in the Hebrew canon. (The "Former Prophets" of the Hebrew Scriptures are included in the "Historical Books" in the Christian Bible.) In this volume the books of the prophets are divided into three units in the order of their appearance in the Protestant canon:

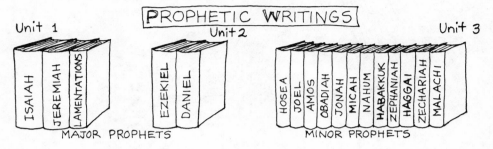

In its general religious sense, prophecy was not restricted to Israel. Neighboring nations also had prophets who claimed to speak for their gods, prophets often in conflict with Israel's prophets. Whatever may have been the character of prophecy among other peoples, in Israel the prophet was one called to be a messenger of God to announce God's word to his people. That word was sometimes warning and judgment, sometimes reassurance and promise. While God's decree called for faith and obedience in the present it often included a future dimension whose effect would appear almost immediately, or in the more distant future (as in New Testament fulfillments) or at the end-time (as in apocalyptic writings).

Although specific messages of the prophets differed, their teachings express an underlying unity grounded in the will of God. Basically they taught what God is like, what God demands of his people, and how God helps his people meet his demands.

As well as can be determined at present, the prophets appear on the world stage as follows:

In Israel

Amos--c. 750 B.C.*
Hosea--c. 745 B.C.

In Judah

Isaiah--740-700 B.C.
Micah--740-700 B.C.
Zephaniah--628-622 B.C.
Jeremiah--628-587 B.C.
Nahum--c. 612 B.C.
Habakkuk--c. 605 B.C.

In Exile

Ezekiel--593-573 B.C.
Obadiah--After 586 B.C.

In Restored Jerusalem

Haggai--520-475 B.C.
Zechariah--520-475 B.C.
Malachi--500-450 B.C.

In Uncertain or Disputed Times

Daniel--Narrative setting and traditional date:
587-538 B.C. Most scholars today:
167-164 B.C. (Maccabean revolt)

Jonah--Narrative setting and traditional date:
783-743 B.C. Most scholars today:
Long after 538 B.C.

Joel--5th or 4th centuries B.C.

Because of the size of their books, these prophets have been called either major or minor. This designation has no relation to the importance of their messages. The "major" prophets are Isaiah, Jeremiah, Ezekiel, and Daniel, while the "minor" prophets comprise one book, "The Twelve," in the Hebrew canon. Jews place Lamentations and Daniel among the "Writings," while the Christian canons place Lamentations after Jeremiah (considered to be its author) and Daniel after Ezekiel.

*Approximate dates are indicated by the use of "c." (Latin "circa"). Dates refer to the persons, not necessarily the books

Reference Maps

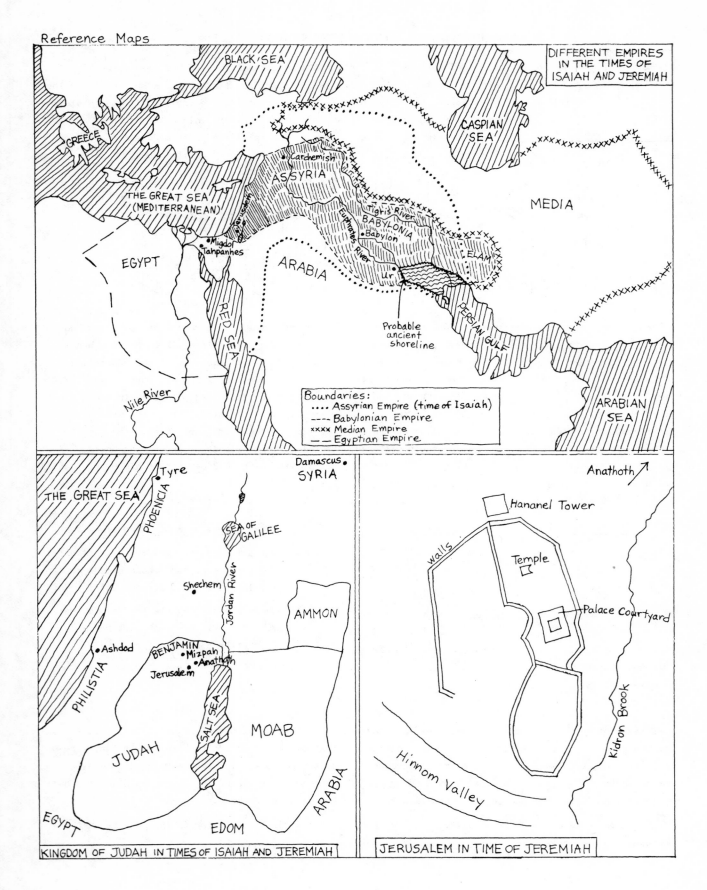

DIFFERENT EMPIRES IN THE TIMES OF ISAIAH AND JEREMIAH

BLACK SEA

GREECE

CASPIAN SEA

THE GREAT SEA (MEDITERRANEAN)

Carchemish

ASSYRIA

MEDIA

Tigris River

BABYLONIA

Babylon

Euphrates River

EGYPT

Migdol
Tahpanhes

ARABIA

ELAM

Ur

PERSIAN GULF

Probable ancient shoreline

RED SEA

Nile River

ARABIAN SEA

Boundaries:
.... Assyrian Empire (time of Isaiah)
---- Babylonian Empire
xxxx Median Empire
–– Egyptian Empire

THE GREAT SEA

Tyre

PHOENICIA

Damascus
SYRIA

SEA OF GALILEE

Shechem

Jordan River

AMMON

Ashdod

BENJAMIN
Mizpah
Jerusalem • Anathoth

PHILISTIA

SALT SEA

MOAB

JUDAH

ARABIA

EGYPT

EDOM

KINGDOM OF JUDAH IN TIMES OF ISAIAH AND JEREMIAH

Anathoth ↗

Hananel Tower

Walls

Temple

Palace Courtyard

Kidron Brook

Hinnom Valley

JERUSALEM IN TIME OF JEREMIAH

4

UNIT 1: ISAIAH, JEREMIAH, AND LAMENTATIONS

OBJECTIVES

In Book 4, items you are to learn have been classified in four
major categories: structure, narrative, prophecy, and features.
"Structure" is basically the outline of each book, taught in
the introduction, elaborated by the numbered headings in the
guided reading, and reinforced by the drawings on questions
pages and by the charts. It also includes sequence of events
in Scripture. "Narrative" includes persons, places, and events
in their relationship to each other. "Prophecy" includes signs
and their meanings and information "about prophecies." "Features"

includes special information about each book given in the introduction, as well as distinctive content,
themes, and quotations from each book. Organization of material into these categories is designed to
help you learn more easily and to know what you are learning.

Upon completion of Unit 1, you will be able to do at least 90% of the following:

1. Give 3 major parts of Isaiah and 5 outline headings for Jeremiah.
2. Arrange 6 events from Isaiah and 5 from Jeremiah chronologically.
3. Associate 10 persons and 10 places with events or characteristics.
4. Identify facts in 5 events given in these three books.
5. State the meaning of 15 signs given in these three books.
6. Identify 10 statements of prophecy, warning, and blessing from these books.
7. State 9 background facts about these books.
8. Identify the source of 8 special content items and 13 well-known or significant quotations.

INSTRUCTIONS

Each page of guided reading in Unit 1 is divided by asterisks into four "frames." DO NOT READ ALL THE WAY
DOWN THE PAGE, but turn the page after reading a single frame. Proceed as follows:

1. Take the Unit 1 pre-test and record your score.
   On this and all tests wording may usually
   vary if the meaning is the same.
2. Study the introduction and outline as you begin
   each book.
3. Note the number and heading of each frame.
4. Read the questions in each frame first.
5. Read the Bible passages assigned. When asked to
   scan a passage, you may skip it, skim over it,
   or read it.
6. Try to answer the questions from memory. Just
   say the answers to yourself. You may write
   them if you wish, but it will double the time
   required.
7. When in doubt, look at the Bible to finish
   answering questions.
8. Then and ONLY THEN turn the page to check your
   answers. Exact wording does not usually matter.

9. Note the drawings to help remember major points.
10. Do the Just for Funs if you enjoy them and
    have time. Be sure to follow the instructions
    at the end of the frame even if you skip them.
11. Use section charts plus outlines to review the
    structure and major themes of each book.
12. Take section tests as instructed, check
    answers and record your scores in the back
    of this book, then return to page 11 to
    begin guided reading for the next biblical
    book.
13. Take the unit test. Check answers and record
    scores.
14. As you check unit test answers, look up the
    references for any questions you miss.
15. Complete the Unit 1 growth record on page 138
    and figure your growth in knowledge of the
    content of Isaiah, Jeremiah, and Lamentations.

Now begin the pre-test for Unit 1 on page 7.

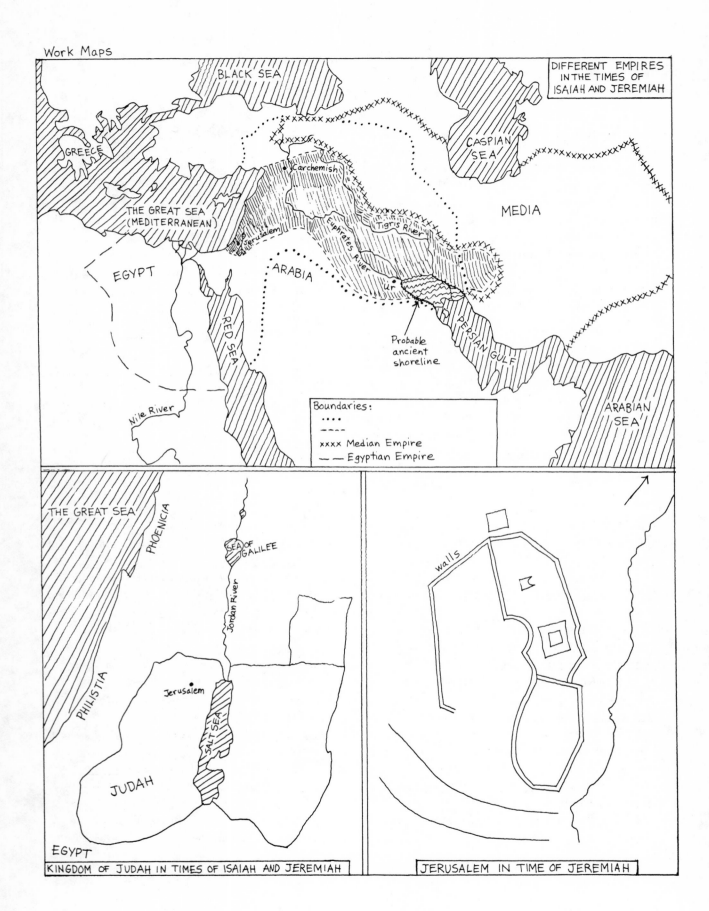

DIFFERENT EMPIRES IN THE TIMES OF ISAIAH AND JEREMIAH

BLACK SEA

GREECE

CASPIAN SEA

Carchemish

MEDIA

THE GREAT SEA (MEDITERRANEAN)

Jerusalem

Tigris River

Euphrates River

EGYPT

ARABIA

Ur

Probable ancient shoreline

PERSIAN GULF

RED SEA

Nile River

ARABIAN SEA

Boundaries:
• • • •
- - - -
xxxx Median Empire
— Egyptian Empire

THE GREAT SEA

PHOENICIA

SEA OF GALILEE

Jordan River

PHILISTIA

Jerusalem

SALT SEA

JUDAH

EGYPT

KINGDOM OF JUDAH IN TIMES OF ISAIAH AND JEREMIAH

walls

JERUSALEM IN TIME OF JEREMIAH

A. STRUCTURE

<u>Outline</u>. Circle the letter of the ONE BEST answer for each.

1. The three major parts of Isaiah in order are:

    a. Hope; Prayer for mercy; Disaster
    b. Warnings; Disaster; Forgiveness
    c. Coming judgment; Hope; Strengthening faith
    d. Call of prophet; Coming judgment; Songs of victory

2. Isaiah Part One begins and ends with:

    a. Warnings and promises; Assyrian threat
    b. Hope; Fall of Jerusalem
    c. Coming judgment; Final judgment
    d. Warnings of doom; Promises of blessing

3. Isaiah Part Two begins and ends with:

    a. War and destruction; Peace and hope
    b. Two faithful servants; Rejection
    c. Good news; Invitation and promise
    d. Conflicts; Reconciliation

4. Isaiah Part Three begins and ends with:

    a. Judgment of the earth; Servant songs
    b. Warnings and promises; Final warnings and promises
    c. The glorious future; Fall of Zion
    d. Comfort; New life

5. Jeremiah begins and ends with:

    a. Conflict with priests; Fulfillment of prophecy
    b. Spiritual struggles; Hope
    c. Judgment; Consolations
    d. Jeremiah's call; Jerusalem's **fall**

6. The major divisions in the body of Jeremiah:

    a. During siege; Last days; Final judgment
    b. Prophet of doom; Conflict; End of time
    c. Jeremiah's life; Prophecies of doom; New life
    d. Prophecies in last reigns; Jeremiah's life; Prophecies against the nations

7. Lamentations is:

    a. Five songs of a sorrowing and fallen city
    b. Four prayers begging for mercy
    c. One long community statement
    d. Cries of the suffering people cursing fate

<u>Sequence</u>. Number these events from 1-10 in the order in which they occurred.

____ Hezekiah shows the Babylonians his military equipment.

____ Cyrus frees the exiles.

____ Assyrians withdraw from attacking Judah.

____ Jehoiakim burns the scroll.

____ Jeremiah is forced to go to Egypt.

____ Ahaz rejects Isaiah's message.

____ Nebuchadnezzar captures Jerusalem again.

____ Isaiah sees the heavenly council.

____ Jehoiachin is exiled.

____ Hezekiah asks Isaiah to pray for Jerusalem.

B. NARRATIVE

<u>Rulers</u>. Write the number of the ruler before the ONE term most closely associated with him.

1. Ahaz
2. Sennacherib
3. Hezekiah
4. Cyrus
5. Jehoiakim
6. Zedekiah
7. Neco
8. Jehoiachin
9. Nebuchadnezzar

____ After Jehudi read to him, he ordered Jeremiah's arrest.

____ Defeated Egypt and Judah

____ Freed and honored after 37 years in prison

____ Told that city would be safe in his time

____ Feared attack by Syria and Israel

____ Egyptian leader

____ God used him to rebuild Jerusalem.

____ Withdrew from the siege of Jerusalem

____ Made false covenant to free slaves

<u>Prophets and Others</u>. Write the number of the person before the ONE term most closely associated with him.

1. Isaiah
2. Jeremiah
3. Hananiah
4. Baruch
5. Ebedmelech
6. Johanan

____ Army officer who did not surrender

____ Scribe who recorded Jeremiah's prophecies

____ Said youth was reason he couldn't speak well

____ Rescued Jeremiah from the well

____ God's presence made him aware of his sin.

____ Proclaimed peace in two years

Places. Write the number of the place before the ONE term that is most closely associated with it.

1. Assyria
2. Babylon
3. Egypt
4. Carchemish
5. Jerusalem
6. Hinnom Valley
7. Temple
8. Ammon
9. Anathoth
10. Syria

_____ With Israel, was plundered by Assyria.

_____ Defeated by Nebuchadnezzar

_____ Cruel despoiler of Jerusalem

_____ Site of Egypt's defeat

_____ Besieged Jerusalem

_____ Hiding place for robbers

_____ Children burned in sacrifice

_____ Trusted the god Milcom

_____ Jeremiah's birthplace

_____ Burned and destroyed in 587 (or 586) B.C.

↓

Events. Circle the letter of the ONE BEST answer.

1. Because people thought the Temple meant safety:

    a. Jeremiah said the Temple would be destroyed.
    b. Jeremiah said being safe required obedience.
    c. Jeremiah said the Temple was not like Shiloh.
    d. a and b

2. Jeremiah almost lost his life through plots by:

    a. Men from Anathoth
    b. People breaking a jar
    c. Officials throwing him in a well
    d. a and c

3. Jeremiah told the exiles to do ALL of these EXCEPT:

    a. Listen to the prophets in Babylon.
    b. Pray for the cities where you live.
    c. Work for your Babylonian cities.
    d. Marry and have children.

4. Jeremiah bought property:

    a. And was arrested as he tried to go to it
    b. As he was nearest of kin
    c. In Benjamin
    d. a, b, and c

5. ALL of the following are true of Jeremiah's scroll EXCEPT:

    a. Jeremiah read it at the Temple.
    b. Jehoiakim cut and burned it.
    c. Baruch recorded Jeremiah's prophecies.
    d. b and c

C. PROPHECY

Signs. Write the number of the sign before its ONE meaning.

1. Immanuel
2. Boiling pot
3. Naked prophet
4. Lord's banquet
5. Almond branch
6. Baskets of figs
7. Quick-loot-fast-plunder
8. The stump

_____ Destruction from the north over Judah

_____ Exiles return, but Jews in Judah and Egypt die

_____ God is with us!

_____ Foolish to trust Egypt and Sudan for help

_____ Assyria will loot Damascus and Samaria.

_____ The Lord is watching.

_____ The Lord will destroy death and disgrace.

_____ A new king from David's family line

Signs (continued).

9. Ruined shorts
10. Bush in desert
11. Tree by stream
12. Ox yoke
13. Potter and clay
14. Stones in Tahpanhes
15. Widow

_____ Jerusalem in sorrow after disgrace and ruin

_____ God placing nations under servitude to Babylon

_____ God will not bless those who disobey.

_____ A person who trusts God

_____ God will spoil his people's pride.

_____ Nebuchadnezzar will defeat Egypt.

_____ A person who turns away from God

About Prophecies. Circle the letter of the ONE BEST answer for each prophecy.

1. The servant songs include the:

    a. Obedient servant
    b. Faithless servant
    c. Servant Israel
    d. a and c

2. The Lord sent the spirit-filled prophet to:

    a. The prisoners
    b. The blind and lame
    c. The poor
    d. a and c

3. ALL of these may be messianic prophecies EXCEPT:

    a. David's descendant will rule perfectly forever.
    b. My people will be taken into exile.
    c. I will remove their chains.
    d. I will make a new covenant.

4. Jeremiah saw ALL of these fulfilled EXCEPT:

   a. God's people will serve foreigners.
   b. God will treat the Temple as he did Shiloh.
   c. The exiles will return to Jerusalem.
   d. Hananiah will die within the year.

5. Jeremiah prophesied ALL of these EXCEPT:

   a. Judah must confess to remove the Lord's anger.
   b. God takes care of his people.
   c. Nebuchadnezzar will spare Jeremiah's friends.
   d. God will spoil the pride of his people.

Write the number of the ONE term before the prophecy most closely associated with it.

6. Eternal rule
7. God's anger
8. Edom
9. Babylon
10. So hard for Judah to stop sinning

_____ Would be punished for their pride.

_____ To be destroyed for thinking it was God.

_____ The Lord will send a new king.

_____ Their fear was greater than their trust in God.

_____ Can a leopard remove its spots?

D. FEATURES

Write 1, 2, or 3 for the three parts of Isaiah; J for Jeremiah; or L for Lamentations before each.

Background.

_____ Exceptionally beautiful poetry

_____ Awareness of sin (major theme)

_____ First in Old Testament to predict harmony in all creation

_____ c. 600 B.C.

_____ Spiritual struggles

_____ c. 700 B.C.

_____ Returned exiles losing faith

_____ Written to encourage the exiles

Special Content.

_____ Suffering servant

_____ Prince of Peace

_____ Road of Holiness

_____ New Exodus

_____ Prophet sorrowing for his people

_____ Symbolic actions

_____ Song of the vineyard

Quotations.

_____ Come, everyone who is thirsty.

_____ Change the way you are living.

_____ The Sovereign Lord has filled me with his spirit.

_____ Prepare in the wilderness a road for the Lord.

_____ Her enemies succeeded; they hold her in their power.

_____ Holy, holy, holy! The Lord Almighty is holy!

_____ Because of our sins he was wounded.

_____ God is with us!

_____ The Sovereign Lord will destroy death forever!

_____ But the Lord is just, for I have disobeyed him.

_____ You will seek me and you will find me.

_____ You are our father, Lord.

_____ Comfort my people.

Check your answers, page 131. Compute your scores, page 136, and enter them on the Unit 1 growth record, page 138. Then begin the study of Isaiah on page 11.

OUTLINES

NOTE: You are asked to memorize all headings except those with a letter after the numeral. To help you learn the outline for each book, structure drawings are used. Each time a new heading is introduced, the structure is built that far. Outlines move from top to bottom within the structure drawings.

INTRODUCTION TO PART ONE (Isaiah 1--39)

The prophet Isaiah lived in Judah, probably Jerusalem, during the last half of the eighth century before Christ (c. 740-700 B.C.). He was active during the reigns of Uzziah, Jotham, Ahaz, and Hezekiah (like "says a LI-ar"), saw the fall of the Northern Kingdom, and announced God's judgment of Jerusalem. Part One represents this time period. (Its historical events are recorded in 2 Kings 15--20 and 2 Chronicles 26--32.)

Called to prophesy to a people who would turn even farther from their Lord as he spoke to them, Isaiah preached doom and disaster, but always reminded his listeners of God's gracious love for his people. Isaiah broke new ground in his preaching on several themes: peace among nations, harmony in all creation, the coming Messiah, and the stump or remnant through whom God would restore Israel.

Study the outline opposite for Part One, and then turn to 10 on the next page.

* * * * * * * * * * * * *

20   INTRODUCTION TO PART TWO (Isaiah 40--55)

Tradition ascribes Part Two to the eighth-century Isaiah who wrote Part One. Because of literary style, historical background, and the absence of the name of Isaiah, a wide consensus of modern scholars concludes that this part was written by a later prophet who announced the return that Isaiah had predicted. This part of the book is sometimes called "Second Isaiah."

The setting for these chapters is the exile in Babylon around 540 B.C., with Jerusalem in ruins and Assyria no longer a power. Babylonia is, but not for long. The prophet announces that Cyrus of Persia is God's instrument, to see that Jerusalem is rebuilt and the Temple is restored.

The poetry in Part Two is universally acclaimed for its great beauty. In it Christians find inspiring prophecies of Jesus Christ as servant of the Lord. These songs of salvation were written to console Israel by announcing the end of the exile and to demonstrate that Israel's God is still acting in history.

Study the outline opposite for Part Two and then turn to 20 on the next page.

* * * * * * * * * * * * *

40   INTRODUCTION TO JEREMIAH

For 41 years (628-587 B.C.) Jeremiah prophesied in Jerusalem and he continued to prophesy in exile. Various compositional techniques, such as common themes, catchwords, or poetic considerations, have determined the arrangement of this book, so that prophecies of different periods are grouped together.

The book of Jeremiah gives both his prophecies and life incidents (especially the spiritual), far more than is given for any other Old Testament prophet. The Lord forbade Jeremiah both marriage and social life, so that he was forced to rely on God alone. Perhaps influenced by this, he stressed the individual's responsibility to God and also the communion possible between God and the individual.

The themes of Jeremiah's prophecies are doom, which can be changed by repentance and sincere faith and obedience. Jeremiah's prophecy of the new covenant, in which a person is given a new heart, became a major New Testament theme.

Study the outline of Jeremiah opposite and then turn to 40 on the next page.

Circle the ONE BEST answer for each of the first three and complete the statement in 4. Then check answers upside down at the end of the frame.

1. Isaiah lived about:
    a. 1000 B.C.
    b. 720 B.C.
    c. 620 B.C.
    d. 510 B.C.
    e. 333 B.C.

2. In Part One Isaiah preached:
    a. God's love for people
    b. Doom and disaster
    c. To those who would not listen
    d. b and c
    e. a, b, and c

3. Isaiah lived at the time of:
    a. The fall of the Northern Kingdom
    b. The fall of Jerusalem
    c. The exile in Babylon
    d. The rebuilding of Jerusalem
    e. a and b

4. New themes in Isaiah's preaching were _____ among _____, _____ in all_____, the _____ _____, and the_____.

Begin guided reading at 11 on the next page.

Answers: 1. b; 2. e; 3. a; 4. peace, nations, harmony, creation, coming Messiah, stump (or remnant)

* * * * * * * * * * * * * *

* * * * * * * * * * * * * *

Complete the following statements about Part Two. Then check your answers with those given upside down.

1. Part Two describes the time of the _____.

2. Isaiah 40--55 is known for its _____ _____.

3. These chapters are written to _____ Israel, and also to demonstrate that Israel's God is still _____ in _____.

4. Christians see the prophecies about the servant of the Lord fulfilled in _____ _____.

Begin guided reading at 21 on the next page.

Answers: 1. exile; 2. beautiful poetry; 3. console (or comfort), acting in history; 4. Jesus Christ

* * * * * * * * * * * * * *

Circle the number of the ONE BEST answer for each. Then check answers upside down.

1. Jeremiah prophesied around:
    a. 800 B.C.
    b. 700 B.C.
    c. 600 B.C.
    d. 500 B.C.
    e. 400 B.C.

2. The book of Jeremiah includes:
    a. A description of Jeremiah's spiritual life
    b. Prophecies of destruction
    c. Prophecies in chronological order
    d. a and b
    e. a, b, and c

3. The theme of Jeremiah's prophecies and preaching is:
    a. Doom that can be changed
    b. A need for repentance
    c. Faith and obedience
    d. a and c
    e. a, b, and c

4. A major prophecy in Jeremiah is about the time when:
    a. God will give new hearts
    b. God will give new laws
    c. Another city will take the place of Jerusalem
    d. a and c
    e. a, b, and c

Begin guided reading at 41 on next page.

Answers: 1. c; 2. d; 3. e; 4. a

PART ONE: THE COMING JUDGMENT (Isaiah 1--39)

11   WARNINGS AND PROMISES (chapters 1--12)

11A About Judah and Jerusalem

   Read Isaiah 1; scan 2--4; read 5.

1. The Lord does not want Israel to sacrifice and observe holy
    days as they have been doing. What does he want?

NOTE: The promise of future peace in Isaiah 2:2-4 is repeated
       in Micah 4:1-3.

2. In the Song of the Vineyard parable, how are the Israelites
    like sour grapes?

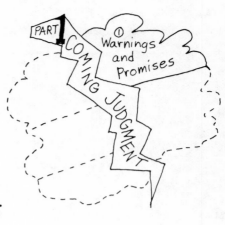

                              Turn to 11A on the next page.

                              * * * * * * * * * * * * *

PART TWO: HOPE FOR THE EXILES (Isaiah 40--55)

21   PROLOGUE: GOOD NEWS!

   Read Isaiah 40:1-11.

1. After the prophet is called to comfort God's people, to pre-
    pare a road for the Lord, what message is he told to
    proclaim?

2. What good news is Jerusalem to proclaim?

NOTE: Verse 3 is quoted in all four Gospels. Compare it with
       the holy voices in chapter 6.

                              Turn to 21 on the next page.

                              * * * * * * * * * * * * *

41   JEREMIAH'S CALL (chapter 1)

   Read Jeremiah 1.

1. When did Jeremiah say he was too young to know how to speak?
2. What were the meanings of the two visions?

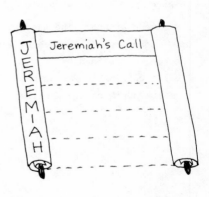

                              Turn to 41 on the next page.

                              * * * * * * * * * * * * *

43E The Sufferings of Jeremiah

   Read Jeremiah 36:1--38:13; scan 38:14-28.

1. Baruch (pronounced like "barrack") recorded Jeremiah's prophecies as Jeremiah dictated. When Jehudi
    (like "a hooty") read the scroll to the king, what did Jehoiakim do?

2. As the Babylonian army retreated from Jerusalem before the advancing Egyptians, what happened to
    Jeremiah who was trying to take possession of the field he had bought in Benjamin?

3. Jeremiah was put in a well for urging the people to surrender to the Babylonians. How did he get
    out?

                              Turn to 43E on the next page.

11A

1. The Lord wants Israel to see that justice is done.

2. They committed murders and treated people unjustly.

Turn to 11B on the next page.

* * * * * * * * * * * *

21

1. People are like grass that withers, but the word of our God endures forever. (Isaiah 40:8)

2. The Lord is coming to rule with power, bringing with him the people he has rescued.

NOTE: These verses 9-11 have been set to music in Händel's <u>Messiah</u>.

Turn to 22 on the next page.

* * * * * * * * * * * *

41

1. He gave this excuse when God called him to be a prophet.

2. The almond branch: The Lord is watching to see that his words come true. (The Hebrew word "watch" is similar to the one for "almond.")
   The pot boiling in the north: "Destruction will boil over from the north on all who live in this land."

Turn to 42 on the next page.

* * * * * * * * * * * *

43E

1. Jehoiakim cut off and burned parts of the scroll as they were read. Then he ordered the arrest of Jeremiah and Baruch.

2. The officer at the city gate arrested, beat, and imprisoned Jeremiah, thinking he was defecting.

3. Ebedmelech (like "we bid REL-ic") got Zedekiah's permission and rescued Jeremiah from the well.

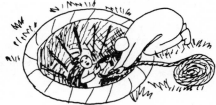

Turn to 43E on the next page.

11B   Isaiah's Call and Testimony
    Read Isaiah 6.

1. What did Isaiah hear, as God's presence made him aware of his sin and made him feel there was no hope for him?

2. After Isaiah had been forgiven and he had volunteered to be the messenger, what message was he told to give to the people?

3. What doom and what hope did the Lord give Isaiah in this vision?

* * * * * * * * * * * * *

22   CONSOLATION OF ISRAEL (chapters 40:12--54:17)
22A   God, Idols, and Israel
    Scan 40:12-26; read 40:27--42:13.

1. After answering Israel's complaints about God, the prophet tells of the Lord's present activity. What is the Lord planning to do in order to send his people back to Zion?

2. For what purpose has the Lord given his servant Israel power?

NOTE: Isaiah 42:1-4 is the first of the four servant songs in Part Two.

JUST FOR FUN! Memorize the well-known verse 40:31.

* * * * * * * * * * * * *

42   PROPHECIES DURING THE REIGNS OF JUDAH'S LAST FOUR KINGS
    (chapters 2--25)
42A   God and Israel's Sin
    Read Jeremiah 2--3.

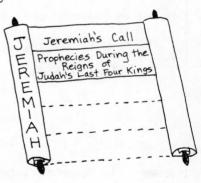

1. No matter what care the Lord showed his people, the people, rulers, priests, and prophets, all rebelled against him. What does the Lord say will punish Israel?

2. What is the great sin Israel and Judah committed?

3. What must Israel and Judah do to remove the Lord's anger?

* * * * * * * * * * * * *

43E   The Sufferings of Jeremiah *(continued)*
    Read Jeremiah 39; scan 40--42; read 43.

4. What happened to Jerusalem and to Jeremiah?

5. How did the leaders respond to Jeremiah's pronouncement of the Lord's answer (not to go to Egypt)?

6. What was the meaning of the stones in Tahpanhes (sounds like "MA can please")?

11B

1. "Holy, holy, holy! The Lord Almighty is holy!"

2. "No matter how much you listen, you will not understand. No matter how much you look, you will not know what is happening."

3. Doom: Judah's cities will be ruined, the people sent away.

   Hope: There will be a stump (a new beginning for God's people).

NOTE: The "Holy, holy, holy..." is often heard in Christian worship. The same words appear in Revelation 4:8.

* * * * * * * * * * * *

22A

1. The Lord plans to bring a man from the east to attack the rulers of Babylon (Cyrus, king of Medes and Persians).

2. The Lord has given his servant power to see that justice is done on earth and through the servant to make a covenant with all peoples and bring light to the nations.

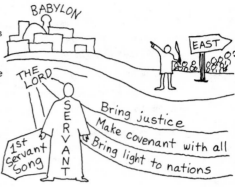

* * * * * * * * * * * *

42A

1. Her own evil will punish Israel.

2. Idolatry (worship of other gods) is the great sin.

3. They must confess their guilt and come back to the Lord.

* * * * * * * * * * * *

43E

4. The Babylonians burned the palace and the homes, tore down the city walls, and took prisoner all but the very poor. Jeremiah, however, was set free.

5. They said Jeremiah was lying and they went to Egypt, taking Jeremiah and Baruch.

6. They were a sign that the Lord would bring Nebuchadnezzar to defeat Egypt.

16

11B   ISAIAH'S CALL AND TESTIMONY *(continued)*
Read Isaiah 7.

4. The attack by Israel and Syria frightened Ahaz of Judah.
    2 Kings tells us he was negotiating an alliance with Assyria.
    The Lord sent Isaiah and his son Shear Jashub ("a few will
    come back") to Ahaz with what message?

5. What sign did the Lord send Ahaz that his message was true?

6. What did Isaiah prophesy to Ahaz then?

8th century B.C.
(740-700 B.C.)

* * * * * * * * * * * * *

22B   Promise: A New Exodus
    Read Isaiah 42:14--43:7.

NOTE: Verses 1-3 in chapter 43 are the basis for the well-known
        hymn "How Firm a Foundation."

1. Why does the Lord call Israel a blind and deaf servant?

2. Why will the Lord bring all his people home?

* * * * * * * * * * * * *

42A   God and Israel's Sin *(continued)*
    Read Jeremiah 4--5; scan 6.

4. When will the kings and officials lose their courage?

5. What pain does Jeremiah find so hard to bear?

6. What will be God's fitting punishment for people who serve
    foreign gods in their own land?

* * * * * * * * * * * * *

43E   The Sufferings of Jeremiah *(continued)*
    Read Jeremiah 44--45.

7. Why did the people say they would worship the Queen of Heaven?

8. When Baruch was depressed what did the Lord tell him?

11B

4. The Lord declares that Israel and Syria are weak and will not take over Jerusalem.

5. The sign: "A young woman who is pregnant will have a son and will name him 'Immanuel'" (Isaiah 7:14). Immanuel means "God is with us." (See footnote in the *Good News Bible*.)

6. Isaiah prophesied that the lands of Israel and Syria will be deserted and the King of Assyria will come.

JUST FOR FUN! Memorize Isaiah 7:14.

* * * * * * * * * * * * *

22B

1. Because Israel found no meaning in the things its people heard and saw

2. To bring him the glory for which he created them

* * * * * * * * * * * * *

42A

4. On the day that Judah is invaded and destroyed

5. The pain of envisioning the disaster that is coming on his countrymen

6. "As they turned away from me and served foreign gods in their own land, so they will serve strangers in a land that is not theirs."

* * * * * * * * * * * * *

43E

7. They had no trouble until they stopped sacrificing to her.

8. "Don't look for special treatment. You will at least escape with your life."

Check the JUST FOR FUN on the next page. Then follow the instructions at the end of its answer page.

11B   Isaiah's Call and Testimony *(continued)*
    Read Isaiah 8:1-15.

7. What message did the Lord send in the sign of Isaiah's newborn
    son, Quick-Loot-Fast-Plunder?

8. Because Judah feared Israel and Syria instead of trusting the
    Lord, what did the Lord say he would do?

"the new thing I am going to do"

* * * * * * * * * * * *

22B   Promise: A New Exodus *(continued)*
    Read Isaiah 43:8-21; scan 43:22--44:20.

3. When the Lord accuses foreign gods of lying, what role is
    Israel summoned to play in the courtroom?

4. The people are reminded of the road the Lord made for them
    through the Red Sea. What are the people to look for now?

* * * * * * * * * * * *

42B   Temple Sermon and Broken Covenant
    Read Jeremiah 7:1--8:3.

NOTE: It is helpful to read Jeremiah 26 before chapter 7 as it
    describes the events surrounding the sermon given in
    chapter 7.

1. Jeremiah told the people that the Temple would be destroyed and
    they would be carried into exile. What did they have to do
    to stay?

2. What does Jeremiah say they have made the Temple?

3. What was happening in Hinnom Valley?

PROPHESIED c. 600 B.C. at end of 7th century (628-587 B.C.)

* * * * * * * * * * * *

JUST FOR FUN!   Jeremiah: Who and Where?

Can **you** identify the situation in Jeremiah that is analogous to these 20th century ones?

<u>The Popular Candidate</u>

The speaker has good news   All land that our foes took
(He's sky-high in the polls):   In two years will be free!
The Reds are gonna lose--   Relax! We're off the hook.
And freedom win its goals!   (The highest source told <u>me</u>!)

Turn to the next page for another situation and for answers.

11B

7. "All the wealth of Damascus (Syria) and all the loot of Samaria (Israel) will be carried off by the king of Assyria."

8. He would send Assyrian forces to attack Judah and sweep through it.

* * * * * * * * * * * *

22B

3. "You are my witnesses."

4. They are to look for the road the Lord is making through the wilderness ("the new thing I am going to do").

* * * * * * * * * * * *

42B

1. "Change the way you are living." (Also, "Be fair in your treatment of one another.")

2. They have made it a hiding place for robbers.

NOTE: Jesus quoted this verse when he drove out those who were buying and selling in the Temple.

3. The people of Judah had built an altar on which they were sacrificing their children in the fire.

* * * * * * * * * * * *

JUST FOR FUN!   Jeremiah: Who and Where?

To Out-of-Work Buggy Makers in 1920

No help in your curse or your fear;
Don't listen to this foolish cheer:
    "Lots of rigs, soon--
    "Your job back by June!"
No, now try a different career!

Answer

The Popular Candidate: Hananiah (Jer. 28:1-4)

Buggy Makers: Jeremiah's advice to exiles
        (Jer. 29:4-9)

You may enjoy writing some 20th century versions of your own for situations in Jeremiah.

Continue with 44 on the next page.

11B   Isaiah's Call and Testimony *(continued)*
      Read Isaiah 8:16--9:7.

9. Isaiah warned against consulting mediums. What had the people been given?

10. "The Lord Almighty is determined to do all this." To what major deed does this refer? What two other things will he do?

JUST FOR FUN! Memorize the inspiring words in Isaiah 9:6 which Christians believe refer to the birth of Jesus Christ. "He will be called ... Prince of Peace."

PROPHESIED 8th century (740 – 700 B.C.)

* * * * * * * * * * * *

22C   Cyrus and the Fall of Babylon
      Read Isaiah 44:21--45; scan 46; read 47; scan 48.

1. What has the Lord done for the people he created to be his servant?

2. What image does the prophet use to show why no human being has a right to tell God what to do?

3. Why does the Lord give Cyrus power to conquer nations?

4. Why will disaster come to Babylon?

Exiles in Babylon: 597–538 B.C.

* * * * * * * * * * * *

42B   Temple Sermon and Broken Covenant *(continued)*
      Scan Jeremiah 8--9; read 10--12.

NOTE: Jeremiah 8:18--9:3 is a moving passage of Jeremiah's sorrow for his people.

4. What is the difference between the gods of other nations and Israel's God?

5. Who wanted to kill Jeremiah for preaching the Lord's message?

6. How did the Lord answer Jeremiah when he complained that dishonest men succeed while Jeremiah loves God?

PROPHESIED c. 600 B.C. at end of **7**th century (628–587 B.C.)

* * * * * * * * * * * *

44   PROPHECIES AGAINST THE NATIONS (chapters 46--51)

NOTE: All these prophecies demonstrate that the God of Israel is the Lord of history, in prophecies of destruction and also of future peace. It may be helpful to look back at Jeremiah 25:15-38, which is on the same subject.

44A   Egypt and Philistia
      Read Jeremiah 46--47.

1. This passage first describes a power-hungry Egypt under the leadership of Neco. Who defeated Egypt at what city?

2. From where will the attack on Philistia come?

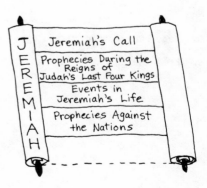

JEREMIAH
Jeremiah's Call
Prophecies During the Reigns of Judah's Last Four Kings
Events in Jeremiah's Life
Prophecies Against the Nations

11B

9. They had Isaiah and his sons as living messages.

10. Major deed: "Prince of Peace...will rule as King David's successor...until the end of time." Any two of these: show the people a great light; give them joy; relieve their burdens; defeat their oppressor.

* * * * * * * * * * * * *

22C

1. The Lord has saved his people by sweeping away their sins.

2. A clay pot doesn't dare complain to the potter or ask what he is doing.

3. The Lord wants Cyrus to free his people Israel and to order Jerusalem to be rebuilt to fulfill God's purpose.

4. Babylon claimed it was God.

* * * * * * * * * * * *

42B

4. Those gods are made of wood and can do nothing. Israel's God is "the living God and the eternal king" who made everything and takes care of his people.

5. The men of Anathoth, Jeremiah's birthplace

6. He warned Jeremiah that there would be far greater trials.

NOTE: Jeremiah 8:22 is often quoted from the King James Version, "Is there no balm in Gilead?"

* * * * * * * * * * * * *

44A

1. Nebuchadnezzar defeated Egypt at Carchemish.

2. From the north

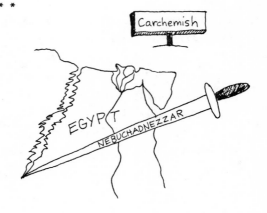

11C   Israel's Fall and Restoration

   Scan Isaiah 9:8-21; read 10--11; scan 12:1-6.

1. The Lord uses the emperor of Assyria to punish those who worship idols. Why then does he say he will punish the emperor?

2. What is the meaning of the stump in Isaiah 11:1?

3. Isaiah describes peaceful and holy Zion under the new king's rule: "The spirit of the Lord will give him wisdom." What does Isaiah prophesy that the Lord will do when the nations gather in Zion to honor the new king?

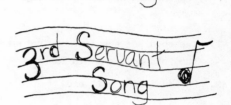

* * * * * * * * * * * * *

22D   Reluctant Servant, Faithful God

   Read Isaiah 49:1--50:3.

What two tasks does the Lord give his servant?

NOTE: Isaiah 49:1-6 is the second servant song.

22E   Obedient Servant, Imminent Rescue

   Read Isaiah 50:4--52:12.

NOTE: Isaiah 50:4-9 is the third servant song.

1. How does the Lord teach his servant to react to insults and beatings?

2. What does the Lord say will happen to suffering Jerusalem?

* * * * * * * * * * * * *

42C   Word Pictures and Symbolic Actions

   Read Jeremiah 13.

1. When Jeremiah found that his shorts were ruined in the hole in the rock, what did the Lord tell him this meant?

2. Jeremiah said that Jerusalem could do nothing but evil. What two questions did he ask to show how hard it would be for Jerusalem to do right?

* * * * * * * * * * * * *

44B   Moab

   Read Jeremiah 48.

What did Moab trust that led to her destruction?

11C

1. The emperor will be punished because of his pride and boasting. He claims he did it all himself.

2. Here branches sprouting from the stump mean "a new king will arise from among David's descendants."

3. The Lord will bring back to his people from other lands.

NOTE: This hymn of thanksgiving in chapter 12 concludes the first major section of the book.

Check the JUST FOR FUN on the next page. Then follow instructions at the end of the JUST FOR FUN answer page.

* * * * * * * * * * * * *

22D

The Lord has appointed his servant to "restore to greatness the people of Israel who have survived" and to be "a light to the nations so that all the world may be saved."

22E

1. The obedient servant does not strike back, but waits for the Lord to prove him innocent.

2. Her suffering will end.

* * * * * * * * * * * *

42C

1. God would spoil the pride of his people. They had not clung to him like a garment. (Note that Babylon was on the Euphrates where Jeremiah hid the shorts.)

2. "Can a black man change the color of his skin, or a leopard remove its spots?"

* * * * * * * * * * * *

44B

Moab trusted her own strength and wealth.

JUST FOR FUN!   Isaiah: Theme Acrostics

This JUST FOR FUN, like all that follow, is for enrichment and enjoyment. Since none are tested, you
may skip any or all of them.

There are many themes in these twelve chapters. You may enjoy making acrostics of them as is done on
the next page. Theme acrostics spell the theme vertically and describe its applications horizontally.
Some themes found in this section are:

DESTROY   SIN   PEACE   CALL   STUMP   IMMANUEL   WARNINGS   PUNISHMENT

PRINCE OF PEACE   NEW KING   RETURN   THANKSGIVING

Turn to the next page for examples of theme acrostics.

* * * * * * * * * * * * *

22F   Suffering Servant, Happy Future
        Read Isaiah 52:13--54:17.

1. Why was the servant beaten and killed?

2. How will God's purpose succeed?

3. "I turned away angry only for a moment." What will the Lord
    do the rest of the time?

JUST FOR FUN! Memorize Isaiah 53:5, which is part of the suffering servant passage that Christians find fulfilled in Jesus Christ.
It expresses the meaning of Christ's death more clearly than any
other Old Testament passage.

NOTE: This entire passage is the fourth and best-known servant song.

* * * * * * * * * * * * *

42C   Word Pictures and Symbolic Actions *(continued)*
        Read Jeremiah 14--15; scan 16; read 17:1-13.

3. After preaching about the coming drought, Jeremiah speaks of
    the prophets who say the Lord has promised peace. What is the
    Lord's answer?

4. Jeremiah is lonely and depressed. Everyone curses him. He
    protests to the Lord that he has loved and obeyed him. What
    does the Lord answer him?

5. Who is like the bush in the desert? the tree by the stream?

* * * * * * * * * * * * *

44C   Smaller Neighbors
        Read Jeremiah 49.

1. Besides their god Milcom, in what did the people of Ammon put their trust, so being led to disaster?

2. What had deceived Edom that led to its destruction?

3. Who were two of the other peoples that the Lord would judge?

JUST FOR FUN Answers

D ragged off as prisoners
E nemies attack
S tealing and looting
T errifying army
R ampaging Assyrians
O dious rulers
Y ou are doomed!

P aths God has chosen are followed
E verlasting peace
A ll disputes among nations settled
C all answered by many
E ager disciples

N o judging by appearances
E verlasting peace in his rule
W isdom from the spirit of the Lord

K nowledge is his
I ntegrity and justice in his rule
N atural world in harmony
G reat light is seen

Continue with guided reading 12 on the next page.

* * * * * * * * * * * * *

22F

1. The Lord's servant was beaten and killed for the sins of the people that the people might be forgiven.

2. Through his servant ("through him my purpose will succeed")

3. The Lord will show Israel his love forever.

Check the JUST FOR FUN on the next page. Then follow instructions at the end of its answer page.

* * * * * * * * * * * * *

42C

3. They are telling lies. He did not send them and they do not know his thoughts. They will die in war.

4. "They will fight against you, but they will not defeat you."

5. The bush in the desert: the person who turns away from God
   The tree by the stream: the person who trusts God

* * * * * * * * * * * * *

44C

1. The people of Ammon trusted their own power.

2. Edom's pride deceived her.

3. Any two of these: Damascus, Kedar, Hazor, Elam

12   JUDGMENT OF NATIONS (chapters 13--23)

12A   Babylon, Assyria, Philistia, Moab

Read Isaiah 13; scan 14--16.

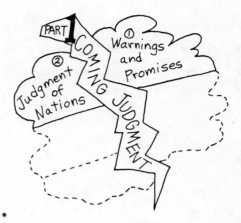

1. On the day of the Lord, what people will be punished by the Lord of Armies for their wickedness?

2. Who will attack Babylonia?

NOTE: The "day of the Lord" refers to God's judgment, whether in history or at the end of the world.

* * * * * * * * * * * * *

JUST FOR FUN!   Isaiah in the New Testament

Isaiah 24:6   "Through you I will bring light to the nations." Can you name one of the three times that someone in the New Testament said that this referred to Jesus?

Isaiah 50:6   "I bared my back to those who beat me. I did not stop them when they insulted me ... and spit in my face." What writer(s) show(s) this prophecy fulfilled?

Isaiah 50:8-9 "God ... will prove me innocent ... himself defends me." Who claims this for God's people?

Isaiah 53:5   "We are healed by the punishment he suffered, made whole by the blows he received." Who said that this referred to Jesus?

Isaiah 53:7-8 "Like a lamb about to be slaughtered...." Who told whom that this was written about Jesus?

Isaiah 53:12   "He ... shared the fate of evil men." Who said this was coming true?

Turn to the next page for answers.

* * * * * * * * * * * * *

42C   Word Pictures and Symbolic Actions *(continued)*

Scan Jeremiah 17:14-27; read Jeremiah 18--19; scan 20.

NOTE: Although not studied here, Jeremiah 20 is a significant chapter. In it Jeremiah is put in stocks and complains to the Lord, but in verse 9 he says that he cannot keep back the Lord's message.

6. What did the Lord teach by the imperfect piece the potter remade?

7. What was the plot against Jeremiah?

8. In chapter 7, verse 31, Jeremiah described the burning of children in Hinnom Valley. What did it mean when Jeremiah broke the clay jar there in front of the priests?

* * * * * * * * * * * * *

44D   Babylon

Scan Jeremiah 50; read 51.

1. What does the Lord do to Babylon?

2. What was the meaning of the book tied to a rock that Seraiah threw into the Euphrates River?

12A

1. The Babylonians will be punished for their wickedness.

2. The Medes will attack Babylon. (The Medes became part of the Persian Empire.)

* * * * * * * * * * * * *

JUST FOR FUN Answers and New Testament References

Isaiah 42:6   Simeon to Mary and Joseph (Luke 2:32; Paul and Barnabas to the Jews (Acts 13:47); or Paul to Agrippa (Acts 26:23)

Isaiah 50:6   Matthew 26:67 and Mark 14:65

Isaiah 50:8-9 Paul (Romans 8:33-34)

Isaiah 53:5   Peter (1 Peter 2:24)

Isaiah 53:7-8 Philip to the Ethiopian official (Acts 8:32-35)

Isaiah 53:12 Jesus (Luke 22:37)

NOTE: For other references to Israel in the New Testament, look through the list of "New Testament Passages Quoted or Paraphrased from the Septuagint" at the back of the *Good News Bible*, pages 367-370.

Continue with guided reading 23 on the next page.
* * * * * * * * * * * * *

42C

6. The people of Israel in the hands of the Lord are like clay in the hands of the potter. He will not bless the people if they disobey him, and he will not punish them when they repent.

7. The people would bring charges against him.

8. The Lord would break the people and the city so they could never be put together again because they would not listen.

Check the JUST FOR FUN! on the next page. Then follow the instructions at the end of its answer page.

* * * * * * * * * * * * *

44D

1. The Lord sends foreigners to destroy Babylon.

2. "Babylonia ... will sink and never rise again because of the destruction that the Lord is going to bring on it."

Check the JUST FOR FUN! on the next page. Then follow the instructions at the end of its answer page.

12B   Syria, Israel, Sudan, Egypt, Babylonia, Edom
        Scan Isaiah 17; read 18--21.

1. After God has punished Sudan and Egypt, what will they both do?

2. What three nations, blessed by God, will in turn bless all the world?

3. What sign shows Judah would be foolish to trust Egypt and Sudan for protection from Assyria?

4. What news will the sentry give when he tells of Babylon's fall?

* * * * * * * * * * * *

23   CONCLUSION: INVITATION AND PROMISE (chapter 55)
        Read Isaiah 55.

The Lord invites his people: "Come, everyone who is thirsty.... "
Then he promises them: "Come to me, and you will have life."
How is God's word like snow and rain?

* * * * * * * * * * * *

JUST FOR FUN!   Political Rulers and Prophets in Jeremiah's Time
Check the "Chronology of the Bible" in the back of your Good News Bible.

1. Who are five kings who ruled during Jeremiah's life as a prophet?

2. What four other prophets were active at the same time?

3. In what year B.C. did the Lord first speak to Jeremiah? (See Jer. 1:2 as well.)

Turn to the next page for answers.

* * * * * * * * * * * *

JUST FOR FUN!   Events in Jeremiah's Life

Across: Down:

1. What Nebuchadnezzar did for Jeremiah when Jerusalem fell.

2. Where he was forced into exile

5. Where Zedekiah put Jeremiah

8. Jeremiah sent this to exiles.

3. Jehoiakim burned it.

4. Jeremiah purchased this.

10. First letters of first two verbs in Israelites' response to the accusation of idolatry (Jer. 44:16)

6. Jerusalem is ____ (abbrev.) of Egypt.

7. Ebedmelech rescued Jeremiah from this.

11. He said many who defended the city would become _____.

9. Jeremiah was brought to ____ for predicting the Temple's destruction.

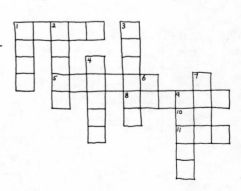

Turn to next page for answers.

12B

1. They will both worship the Lord.

2. Egypt, Assyria, and Israel will be a blessing to the world.

3. The sign of the naked prophet representing the African prisoners led into exile by Assyria

4. Idols lie shattered on the ground.

* * * * * * * * * * * * *

23

"It will do everything I send it to do." (The Lord will give Israel honor and glory, all the blessings promised to David.)

Study the outline of Isaiah Part Two on page 10, and Part Two of Section Chart 1 on page 45. Then take Section Test 2 on page 49.

* * * * * * * * * * * *

JUST FOR FUN Answers

1. Josiah, Joahaz, Jehoiakim, Jehoiachin, and Zedekiah

2. Zephaniah, Nahum, Habakkuk, and Ezekiel

3. 627 or 626 B.C.

Places Mentioned in Jeremiah

Add to the map on page 6 by checking the location of the following places on the map, page 4.
Anathoth and Benjamin (Jer. 1:1; 11:21)
Hinnom Valley (Jer. 7:31. Look at the map of Jerusalem.)

Continue with guided reading 42D on the next page.

* * * * * * * * * * * * *

JUST FOR FUN Answers

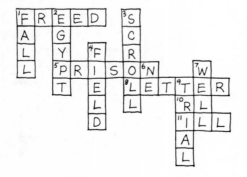

Places Mentioned in Jeremiah

By checking the maps on page 4, add to your maps, page 6, the following places mentioned in Jeremiah: Shiloh (Jer. 26:6; 41:5); Kidron Brook (Jer. 31:40); Hananel Tower (Jer. 31:28); Palace courtyard (Jer. 32:2); Mizpah (Jer. 40:6); Moab, Ammon, Edom (Jer. 40:11); Shechem (Jer. 41:4-5); Migdol, Tahpanhes (Jer. 44:1).

Continue with guided reading 45 on the next page.

12C   Jerusalem and Phoenicia

    Read Isaiah 22--23.

1. What evil would the Lord never forgive those in Jerusalem as the city fell?

2. When Tyre's seventy-year punishment was over, what would happen to the money she earned?

* * * * * * * * * * * * *

30   INTRODUCTION TO PART THREE (Isaiah 56--66)

Part Three has also been traditionally ascribed to the 8th century Isaiah. All known complete manuscripts of the book of Isaiah include all 66 chapters. Some modern scholars consider chapters 56--66 to be the work of the anonymous prophet who may have written Part Two. Many others consider it to be a collection of various similar prophecies, added to Part Two after the exile. It is sometimes called "Third Isaiah."

These chapters were written to the people who had returned to Jerusalem under Cyrus's edict, about 538 B.C. The desolation that greeted them there had made them doubt that God would keep his promises to them. The purpose of these chapters was to turn the people from false worship to the true God once more. They were written to reassure the people that God keeps his promises, and to give them direction in reestablishing the religious and ethical life of God's covenant community.

* * * * * * * * * * * * *

42D   Prophet and King

    Scan Jeremiah 21; read 22:1--23:8; scan 23:9-40; read 24.

1. How could the king and his men change the prophecy of doom?

2. At this point Jeremiah gives messages concerning the last king of Judah. Why will God's judgment be so hard on most of the rulers?

3. Jeremiah 23:5-8 contains a messianic prophecy. What will the king be called?

4. What was the meaning of the baskets of figs?

* * * * * * * * * * * * *

45   THE FALL OF JERUSALEM (chapter 52)

    Read Jeremiah 52.

1. After capturing Jerusalem, what did the Babylonians do to the Temple?

2. What happened to the High Priest and other important men from Jerusalem?

3. What happened to Jehoiachin after 37 years as a prisoner in Babylon?

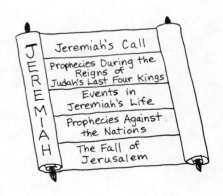

12C

1. They forgot God and celebrated on the housetops because "tomorrow we'll be dead."

2. The money would be dedicated to the Lord. It would buy food and clothing for the worshipers who are in need.

Check the JUST FOR FUN! on the next page. Then follow instructions at the end of its answer page.

* * * * * * * * * * * * *

30   INTRODUCTION TO PART THREE (Isaiah 56--66)

Complete the following statements about Part Three. Then check the answers below, upside down.

1. Part Three describes the time of the _____ to _____.

2. God's people _____ God's _____.

3. These chapters were written to _____ the people and to give them direction in reestablishing the _____ and _____ life of God's covenant community.

Answers: 1. return, Jerusalem 2. doubted, promises; 3. reassure, religious, ethical

* * * * * * * * * * * * *

42D

1. They could change it by doing what is just and right for their people.

2. They have destroyed and scattered God's people and they have worshiped other gods.

3. The Lord Our Salvation

4. Good figs: those taken to Babylon (The Lord will bring them back to Judah.)
   Bad figs: those who stayed in Judah or who moved to Egypt (The Lord will destroy them.)

THE LORD OUR SALVATION

Jews to Babylon — GOOD FIGS

Jews in Judah or to Egypt — BAD FIGS

* * * * * * * * * * * * *

45

1. They burned down the Temple and took away the bronze, silver, and gold.

2. They were all killed.

3. He was freed and honored above other kings in exile with him.

JERUSALEM

JEHOIACHIN

In Babylon

Turn to 50 on the next page and begin your study of Lamentations.
Section Test 5 will include Jeremiah 26--52 and Lamentations.

JUST FOR FUN!   Isaiah's World

The world of Isaiah was very different from that of Jesus' day as well as different from ours. At the time of his call to be a prophet, the great world empire was Assyria. Israel, the Northern Kingdom, was still a nation and a threat to Judah. Amos, Hosea, and Micah were Isaiah's contemporaries.

Using the map on page 4 for reference, locate the places listed on the next page on the blank map on page 6. You may want to review the judgment pronounced on each nation or city in chapters 14 through 23, or to note the twentieth-century names.

Turn to the next page for the list of places.

* * * * * * * * * * * * *

PART THREE: STRENGTHENING THE FAITH OF THOSE WHO RETURN

31   WARNINGS AND PROMISES (chapters 56--59)
        Read Isaiah 56:1-8; scan 56:9-12; read 57.

1. No longer will circumcised Jews be God's only people. What two new groups are going to be welcomed by the Lord in Jerusalem?

2. The Lord promises peace and rest in death for those who live good lives. Sinners worship fertility gods and offer children in sacrifice. What does the Lord say he will do when these sinners cry to their gods in need?

* * * * * * * * * * * * *

42E   Conclusion
        Read Jeremiah 25.

1. How long will Judah and neighboring nations serve Babylon?

2. What will happen to Babylon after that period is up?

* * * * * * * * * * * * *

50   INTRODUCTION TO LAMENTATIONS

All five songs that comprise Lamentations mourn the ruin of Jerusalem following its fall to the Babylonians. The book's major themes are awareness of sin and approval of God's judgment.

The book of Lamentations was anonymous in the Hebrew scriptures and appeared there among the Writings. The Septuagint added a statement attributing Lamentations to Jeremiah. Modern scholars agree that it was written in Jeremiah's time, whether or not by the prophet himself.

These songs, which comprise one of the five Festival Scrolls in the Jewish canon, are sung at the annual Jewish commemoration of the fall of Jerusalem in 587 B.C. (or 586, an insignificant difference).

Babylon   Assyria   Damascus   Elam   Arabia   Tyre   Ashdod   Moab   Syria   Edom

Continue with 13 on the next page.

* * * * * * * * * * * *

31

1. Converted foreigners and eunuchs will also be welcomed to worship the Lord. "My Temple will be called a house of prayer for the people of all nations."

2. He will let them wait for their gods to save them. (He will wait until they turn to him.)

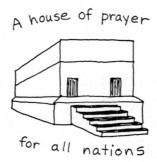

A house of prayer

for all nations

* * * * * * * * * * * *

42E

1. They will serve 70 years.

2. The Lord will punish Babylonia with all the disasters he had threatened to bring on other nations.

NOTE: "This book" in 25:13 probably refers to the early collection of Jeremiah's prophecies of doom and judgment in chapters 2--25.

BABYLON

70 years

BABYLON

Study the outline of Jeremiah 1--25 on page 10, and the chart on page 46. Then take Section Test 4, page 51.

* * * * * * * * * * * *

50   INTRODUCTION TO LAMENTATIONS

Complete the following statements about Lamentations.   Then check answers below, upside down.

1. There are _____ songs in Lamentations.

2. Lamentations shows sorrow for the _____ of _____,

3. and approval of _____'s _____.

4. Lamentations is _____

5. at the _____ Jewish _____

6. of this destruction in _____ B.C.

Answers: 1. Five; 2. destruction (fall) of Jerusalem; 3. God's judgment; 4. sung; 5. annual, commemoration; 6. 587 (or 586)

13   JUDGMENT OF THE EARTH (chapters 24--27)

   Read Isaiah 24:1--25:10; scan 26:1-18; read 26:19-21; scan 27.

NOTE: These chapters depict the last judgment. You might
        compare them with the Revelation to John in the New
        Testament.

1. After punishing the earth for its sins, the Lord will give a
    banquet for all nations. What will God do that will make
    everyone call him Lord?

2. What will happen to those who hid their crimes?

* * * * * * * * * * * *

31   WARNINGS AND PROMISES *(continued)*

   Read Isaiah 58--59.

3. What kind of fasting does the Lord want from his people?

4. Why didn't God answer the prayers of the people as they begged God for help and tried to worship him?

* * * * * * * * * * * *

43   EVENTS IN JEREMIAH'S LIFE (chapters 26--45)

43A   Trial and Acquittal

   Read Jeremiah 26.

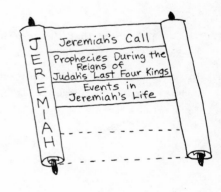

1. The Temple sermon referred to here is given in chapter 7. Why
    did the priests and prophets want to sentence Jeremiah to
    death?

2. What did the elders recall about Hezekiah's reign that made
    them spare Jeremiah's life?

* * * * * * * * * * * *

51   THE SORROWS OF JERUSALEM

   Read Lamentations 1.

1. Who is like a widow and why?

2. What do the people of this ruined city think of God's having
    carried out such destruction?

NOTE: The first four of the five songs of Lamentations are alpha-
        betical psalms, 1, 2, and 4 taking the form of a dirge for
        the dead.

13

1. "The Sovereign Lord will destroy death forever! He will wipe away the tears from everyone's eyes and take away the disgrace his people have suffered throughout the world." (Only the first statement need be given to be correct.)

2. Their murders will be revealed.

* * * * * * * * * * * *

31

3. The Lord wants his people to end injustice and oppression; to share their food, shelter, and clothing with those in need. (Any two will do.)

4. Their sins separate them from God.

* * * * * * * * * * * *

43A

1. Jeremiah declared that the Lord intended to treat the Temple as he had Shiloh (like HIGH-low) if the people did not repent.

2. Micah (like MIKE-uh) had predicted destruction for Jerusalem and the Temple, but Hezekiah tried to please the Lord, so the Lord relented.

* * * * * * * * * * * *

51

1. Jerusalem is like a widow because "her enemies ... hold her in their power. The Lord has made her suffer for all her many sins."

2. "The Lord is just for I have disobeyed him."

"...for I have disobeyed him."

14   MORE WARNINGS AND PROMISES (chapters 28--35)

14A   About Samaria and Jerusalem
    Read Isaiah 28--29; scan 30--32.

1.   Of what sin does Isaiah accuse both national leaders and prophets?

2.   Jerusalem's destruction is prophesied. How does the Lord describe the religious people in Jerusalem?

3.   "You didn't make me." "You don't know what you are doing." Who are like the potter and the clay?

* * * * * * * * * * * *

32   SALVATION SONGS (chapters 60--62)
    Scan Isaiah 60; read 61--62.

1.   The Lord fills the prophet with his spirit to send him to help certain groups of people. Who are four of these groups?

2.   The Lord announces that he's bringing the people to Jerusalem. What are two of the titles that he gives Jerusalem?

* * * * * * * * * * * *

43B   A Pamphlet for Exiles
    Read Jeremiah 27--29.

1.   What was the meaning of the ox yoke that Jeremiah wore when he gave his messages to the foreign kings conferring with Zedekiah (ch. 27)?

2.   What was the warning to those who wanted to resist (ch. 27)?

3.   In the Temple what did Hananiah (like "Ham 'n RYE...uh") claim that the Lord had told him to say (ch. 28)?

4.   What prediction did Jeremiah make about Hananiah that came true in a few months (ch. 28)?

5.   To whom did Jeremiah write, saying to build homes, to marry and have children, and to pray and work for the good of the cities where they lived (ch. 29)?

* * * * * * * * * * * *

52   THE PUNISHMENT OF JERUSALEM
    Read Lamentations 2.

How has the Lord punished Jerusalem?

14A

1. He accuses them both of drunkenness.

2. Their religion is made up of meaningless memorized rules and traditions made by human beings.

3. The Lord is the potter. Those he created are the clay.

* * * * * * * * * * * * *

32

1. The poor, the broken-hearted, captives and prisoners, and those who mourn. (Jesus quoted this passage as being fulfilled in him in Luke 4:16-30.)

2. God Is Pleased with Her (Hephzibah in King James); Happily Married (Beulah); God's Holy People; The People the Lord Has Saved; The City That God Loves; The City That God Did Not Forsake (Any two will do.)

* * * * * * * * * * * * *

43B

1. The servitude to Babylonia in which God was placing all nations would continue for their children and grandchildren until Babylon fell.

2. Those who did not submit would be punished with war and disease until destroyed, but those who surrendered would save their lives.

3. Within two years God would bring back the Temple treasures, the king and the exiles.

4. Hananiah would die for telling the people to rebel against God.

5. The Jewish exiles in Babylon.

* * * * * * * * * * * *

52

He tore it down and destroyed it.

14B   The Last Judgment and Restoration
         Read Isaiah 33; scan 34; read 35.

PROPHESIED 740-700 B.C.

1. The prophet speaks of a day of great peace and joy with free-
    dom from oppression by foreigners. Who will be king at that
    time?

2. After describing the horror of the last judgment, Isaiah
    contrasts it with the life of his people who return. Where
    does the Road of Holiness lead?

3. Name at least three things that will happen to the people who
    travel this road.

* * * * * * * * * * * * *

33   FINAL WARNINGS AND PROMISES (chapters 63--66)
         Read Isaiah 63:1-6; scan 63:7-14; read 63:15--64:12.

1. Why was the Lord's clothing red?

2. In this prayer the people wish God would reveal his power as
    in past ages. They acknowledge their sin and ask that it not
    be held against them forever. Why do they say God should
    help them?

* * * * * * * * * * * * *

43C   The Book of Consolation
         Read Jeremiah 30--31.

1. When the terrible day comes, what will the Lord do?

2. What is the source of bitter weeping?

3. What will the Lord do for his people in the future, working as
    hard as he did to destroy them?

4. What is this new covenant that will replace the old Sinai
    covenant?

PROPHESIED 628-587 B.C.

* * * * * * * * * * * * *

53   PUNISHMENT AND HOPE
         Read Lamentations 3.

What does the suffering prophet recall that renews hope within him?

54   JERUSALEM IN RUINS
         Read Lamentations 4.

Reduced to living among the rubble and starving to death, what
atrocity did mothers commit?

14B

1. "The Lord himself will be our king."

2. It leads to Jerusalem (Zion).

3. At least three of the following:
   The tired and weak will be strengthened and encouraged;
   the blind will see; the deaf will hear; the lame will leap;
   the mute will shout.

NOTE: Jesus quoted this passage, together with Isaiah 61:1, as
       evidence to John that he was the Messiah (Matt. 11:5;
       Luke 7:22).

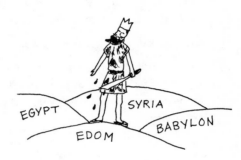

* * * * * * * * * * * * *

33

1. To save his people he had trampled the nations, their blood
   staining his clothes.

2. One of these answers will do:
   "You are our father, Lord." (Note the father image.)
   "You created us." (Note the potter and clay image.)
   "We are your people."

* * * * * * * * * * * * *

43C

1. He "will break the yoke ... and remove their chains."

2. "Rachel is crying for her children."

3. He will take just as much care to plant them and build them
   up. They will have their own land and food, and will know
   joy and peace again.

4. God will put his law within his people, writing it on their
   hearts; all will know him and he will forgive their sins.
   (This is considered a messianic prophecy.)

* * * * * * * * * * * * *

53

"The Lord's unfailing love and mercy still continue."
"The Lord ... will not reject us forever."

54

"Loving mothers boiled their own children for food."
(Also mentioned in verse 20 of chapter 2)

15   THE ASSYRIAN THREAT (chapters 36--39)

  Read Isaiah 36--37; scan 38; read 39.

NOTE: With few changes Isaiah 36--39 is the same as 2 Kings
       18:13--20:19.

1. When Sennacherib (sounds like "suh MACK a rib) took cities of
    Judah and threatened Jerusalem, Hezekiah (like "says ... uh
    ... LI-ar") asked Isaiah to pray for Jerusalem. How did
    Isaiah say that the Lord answered him?

2. What happened to the Assyrians?

3. After Hezekiah showed the Babylonians all his treasure and
    military equipment, what did Isaiah prophesy?

* * * * * * * * * * * * *

33   FINAL WARNINGS AND PROMISES *(continued)*

  Read Isaiah 65; scan 66.

PROPHESIED to the Jews who returned to Jerusalem

3. The Lord was ready to answer his people's prayers. Why didn't
    he?

4. "I am making a new earth and new heavens." The Lord describes
    many blessings that he will give to those who worship him in
    the new Jerusalem. Can you recall at least three?

NOTE: The New Creation theme of chapter 65:17-25 parallels the
       themes of the peaceful kingdom in Isaiah 11, the glorious
       future in Isaiah 33, the new exodus in chapter 43, the
       promises of chapter 44, and the restored Jerusalem of
       chapters 49 and 51.

* * * * * * * * * * * * *

43C   The Book of Consolation *(continued)*

  Read Jeremiah 32--33.

5. Jehoiachin (like "en-JOY a spin"), rulers, priests, and people were already in exile, and Jerusalem
    was under siege by Nebuchadnezzar again. At this time, what did Jeremiah do (as nearest of kin) that
    dramatized the eventual new life in Judah?

6. When Jeremiah was in prison the Lord gave him another message. Who would the Lord always choose to
    rule over his people?

* * * * * * * * * * * * *

55   A PRAYER FOR MERCY

  Read Lamentations 5.

Proclaiming that the Lord is king forever, what do the people in
Jerusalem beg him to do?

15

1. The Lord would send a rumor which would take Sennacherib back to Assyria where he would be killed. Jerusalem would be safe from the Assyrians.

2. The Lord sent an angel who killed the Assyrian soldiers and Sennacherib withdrew.

3. All Hezekiah had shown the Babylonians and some of Hezekiah's direct descendants would be carried off to Babylon.

Check the JUST FOR FUN on the next page and then follow directions on its answer page.

* * * * * * * * * * * * *

33

3. They did not pray.

4. Happiness; no weeping or cries for help; no deaths of babies; all to live a full life span (over a hundred); enjoyment of things worked for; successful work; no disasters for children; prayers answered while praying

Check the JUST FOR FUN! on the next page and then follow the instructions on its answer page.

* * * * * * * * * * * * *

43C

5. He purchased property in Benjamin (a field in Anathoth) in the presence of witnesses.

6. He will choose one of David's righteous descendants. (Note that then Jerusalem will be called "The Lord Our Salvation.")

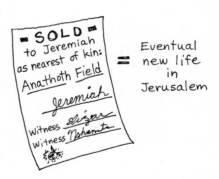

* * * * * * * * * * * * *

55

"Bring us back to you Lord.... Restore our ancient glory."

Back with God

Check the JUST FOR FUN on the next page and then follow the directions on its answer page.

JUST FOR FUN!   Isaiah Part One: Riddles

1. For what reason might a mortician call God his enemy?

2. Who celebrated like a party host who quotes the King James Version, saying, "Eat, drink, and be merry!"?

3. How can "Quick-Food-Fast-Wonder" remind you of Isaiah's family?

4. What does the Road of Holiness have in common with the song "_____, Sweet _____" by John Howard Payne?

5. In Isaiah, how was Egypt like a Chinese New Year celebration?

Turn to the next page for answers.

* * * * * * * * * * * * *

JUST FOR FUN!   Isaiah Part Three: Well-Known Quotations

Can you find verses that are analogies or appropriate in some other way to the following statements?

1. The water table is extremely low. The reservoir went dry two days ago. (Is. 55)

2. Thought and action: by God, by you and me. (Is. 55)

3. Order out the maintenance crews and the road construction gangs! The people made homeless by the flood must be helped to return. (Is. 57)

4. The war on crime is on! The murderers, robbers, and porno kings will never be safe! (Is. 57)

5. They live in a windowless, enclosed city, using electricity instead of the sun and moon. (Is. 60)

6. The unemployed are given jobs, the sad are made glad, and those in prison are freed. (Is. 61)

Turn to the next page for answers.

* * * * * * * * * * * * *

43D   Miscellaneous Episodes
       Read Jeremiah 34; scan 35.

1. During the siege of Jerusalem, King Zedekiah (like "set it HIGH-er") and the people made a covenant with God to try to change his plan of destruction. What was the covenant?

2. Why was God angry with them after that?

* * * * * * * * * * * * *

JUST FOR FUN!   Lamentations and the Crucifixion

Look at Lamentations 1:12. This verse, in the words of the King James Version of the Bible, has been placed on the lips of Jesus in a well-known oratorio about the crucifixion. Who is the composer? Can you sing the words as they are heard there?

Turn to the next page for the answer.

JUST FOR FUN Answers

1. According to God's promise to destroy death forever, he will put morticians out of business (Is. 25:8)!

2. The people of Jerusalem when their city was attacked (Is. 22:13).

3. It rhymes with Isaiah's second son's name, Quick-Loot-Fast-Plunder (Is. 8:3).

4. The song is called "Home, Sweet Home," and that is where the Road of Holiness leads (Is. 35:9).

5. The Chinese New Year is celebrated with a "harmless dragon," the nickname that the Lord gave Egypt in Isaiah 30:7.

Study the outline of Isaiah Part One on page 10, and the first part of Section Chart 1 on page 45. Then take Section Test 1 on page 47.

* * * * * * * * * * * * *

JUST FOR FUN Answers

1. Isaiah 55:1   "Come everyone who is thirsty--here is water!"

2. Isaiah 55:8-9 "My thoughts," says the Lord, "are not like yours, and my ways are different from yours."

3. Isaiah 57:14 "Let my people return to me. Remove every obstacle from their path! Build the road and make it ready!"

4. Isaiah 57:21 "There is no safety for sinners," says the Lord.

5. Isaiah 60:19 "No longer will the sun be your light by day, or the moon be your light by night. I, the Lord, will be your eternal light."

6. Isaiah 61:1 "The Sovereign Lord ... has chosen me ... to bring good news to the poor, to heal the broken-hearted...."

JUST FOR FUN make some of these quotations your own by memorizing them.

Study the outline of Isaiah Part Three, page 10, and the third part of Section Chart 1 on page 45. Then take Section Test 3, page 50.

* * * * * * * * * * * * *

43D

1. To obey God by freeing all their Hebrew slaves

2. They broke this covenant too, forcing the freed slaves to be slaves again.

COVENANT:
FREE ALL SLAVES
Zedekiah

Continue the study of Jeremiah with 43E on page 13.

* * * * * * * * * * * * *

JUST FOR FUN Answer

Sir John Stainer put the words, "Is it nothing to you, all ye that pass by?" to the following melody:

Study the outlines of Jeremiah 26--52 and Lamentations on page 10, and Section Chart 2 on page 46. Then take Section Test 5 on page 52.

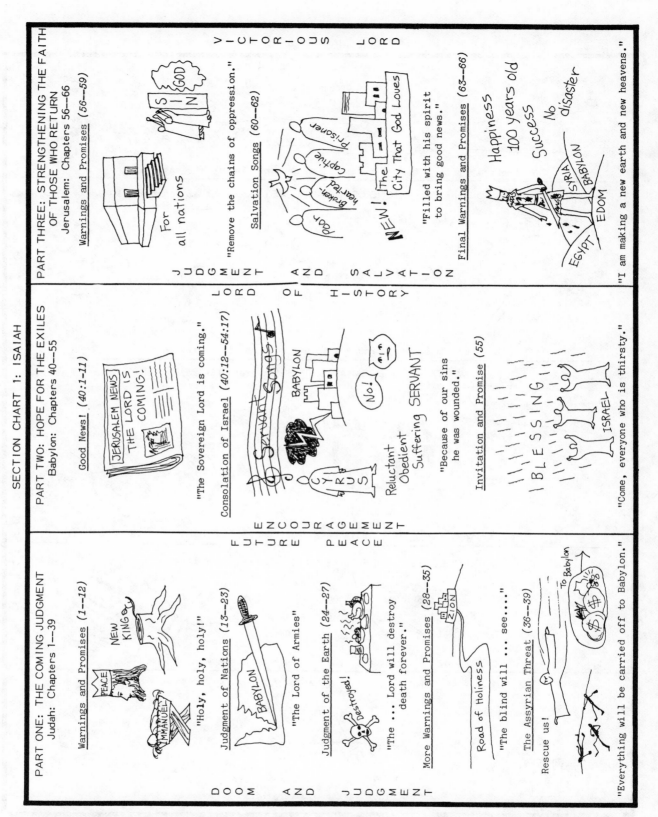

SECTION CHART 1: ISAIAH

PART ONE: THE COMING JUDGMENT
Judah: Chapters 1—39

Warnings and Promises (1—12)

NEW KING
PEACE
IMMANUEL

"Holy, holy, holy!"

Judgment of Nations (13—23)

BABYLON

"The Lord of Armies"

Judgment of the Earth (24—27)

Destroyed!

"The ... Lord will destroy death forever."

More Warnings and Promises (28—35)

ZION

Road of Holiness

"The blind will ... see....."

The Assyrian Threat (36—39)

Rescue us!

To Babylon
$

"Everything will be carried off to Babylon."

DOOM AND JUDGMENT

PART TWO: HOPE FOR THE EXILES
Babylon: Chapters 40—55

Good News! (40:1-11)

JERUSALEM NEWS
THE LORD IS COMING!

"The Sovereign Lord is coming."

Consolation of Israel (40:12—54:17)

Servant Songs
BABYLON
CYRUS
No!

Reluctant
Obedient
Suffering SERVANT

"Because of our sins he was wounded."

Invitation and Promise (55)

BLESSING
ISRAEL

"Come, everyone who is thirsty."

FUTURE ENCOURAGEMENT AND PEACE

LORD OF HISTORY

PART THREE: STRENGTHENING THE FAITH
OF THOSE WHO RETURN
Jerusalem: Chapters 56—66

Warnings and Promises (56—59)

SIN
GOD

For all nations

"Remove the chains of oppression."

Salvation Songs (60—62)

poor
Broken-hearted
captive
Prisoner

NEW! The City That God Loves

"Filled with his spirit to bring good news."

Final Warnings and Promises (63—66)

Happiness
100 years old
Success
No disaster

SYRIA
BABYLON
EGYPT
EDOM

"I am making a new earth and new heavens."

VICTORIOUS LORD

JUDGEMENT AND SALVATION

Study Part One of chart before taking Section Test 1, page 47. Study Part Two before taking Section Test 2, page 49, and Part Three before taking Section Test 3, page 50. Study complete chart before taking Unit Test 1, page 53.

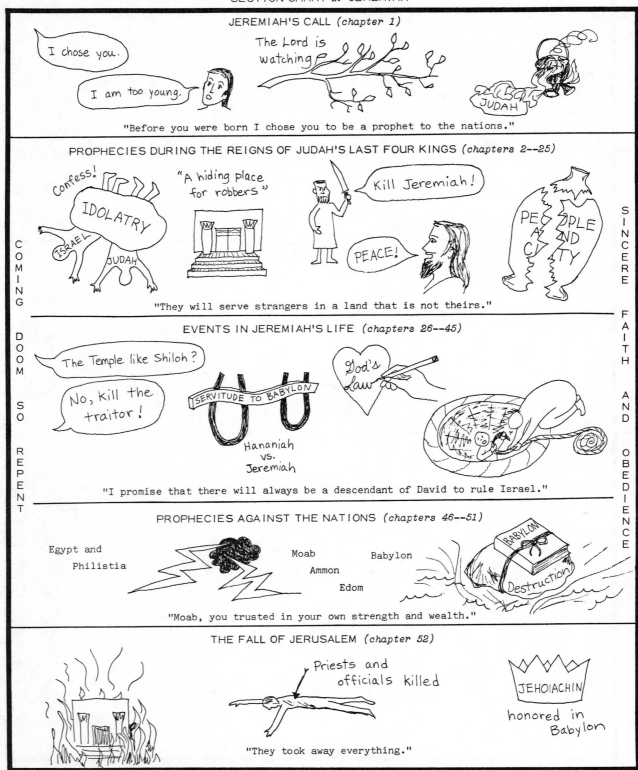

Study the top part of this chart and then take Section Test 4 on page 51. Study the bottom part of the chart and then take Section Test 5, page 52. Study complete chart before taking Unit Test 1 on page 53.

A. STRUCTURE

<u>Outline</u>. Complete this outline of Isaiah Part One.

1. Part One: The _____ _____
2. _____ and _____
3. _____ of _____
4. _____ of the _____
5. More _____ and _____
6. The _____ _____

<u>Sequence</u>. Number the following events from 1-4 in order of their occurrence in Isaiah 1--39.

____ Syrians and Israelites frightened Ahaz.

____ Hezekiah showed Babylonians his treasures.

____ Isaiah was called to be a prophet.

____ Sennacherib defeated cities in Judah.

↓

B. NARRATIVE

<u>Persons</u>. Write the number of EACH person before the ONE term most closely associated with it.

1. Assyrian emperor
2. Shear Jashub
3. Sennacherib
4. Hezekiah
5. Isaiah
6. Ahaz

____ Did not carry out his attack on Jerusalem

____ Was told his descendants would be exiles

____ Afraid of attack by two neighbors

____ To be punished for saying <u>he</u> did these things

____ Said he was doomed for his sin

____ Isaiah's son

<u>Places</u>. Write the number of EACH place before the ONE term most closely associated with it.

1. Judah
2. Media
3. Assyria
4. Babylon
5. Jerusalem
6. Egypt; Sudan
7. Israel and Syria

____ Officials saw Judah's military equipment

____ Used by the Lord to punish idolatrous nations

____ Trusted by Judah for protection from Assyria

____ Feared by Judah

____ Would attack Babylon

____ Nation where Isaiah prophesied

____ People celebrated while under siege

C. PROPHECY

<u>Signs</u>. Write the number of the sign before its meaning.

1. The stump
2. Quick-Loot-Fast-Plunder
3. A child is born!
4. The naked prophet
5. The Lord's banquet
6. Immanuel

____ Foolish to expect help from Egypt and Sudan.

____ God is with us!

____ David's descendant will rule till the end of time.

____ The Lord will destroy death.

____ A new beginning for God's people.

____ Assyria will plunder Syria and Israel.

<u>About Prophecies</u>. Circle the number of the ONE BEST answer for each prophecy.

1. When Isaiah saw the Lord "high and exalted," he was told ALL of the following EXCEPT:

   a. The king would see the Lord acting in events.
   b. The cities of Judah would be ruined.
   c. The people of Jerusalem would be exiled.
   d. The people would not understand.

2. Isaiah reports that the Lord became angry with his people for ALL of these reasons EXCEPT:

   a. They committed murders.
   b. They forgot the Lord when attacked.
   c. They imprisoned his prophet Isaiah.
   d. They were drunkards.

3. Through Isaiah the Lord promised his people to:

   a. Send David's descendant to free them from Babylon
   b. Send a new king to rule forever
   c. Bring the dead to life
   d. b and c

4. Concerning Jerusalem, Isaiah prophesied ALL of the following EXCEPT:

   a. Jerusalem would be destroyed.
   b. The Lord would bring back his people.
   c. The Lord would prepare special garments for the leaders of his people.
   d. Rescued people would reach Jerusalem by the Road of Holiness.

5. The song of the vineyard was ALL of the following EXCEPT:

   a. A parable
   b. About a festival
   c. About sour grapes
   d. About a good farmer

6. When Tyre's punishment is over, her money will be:

   a. Dedicated to the Lord
   b. Used for needy worshipers
   c. Given to Judah
   d. a and b

D. FEATURES

Background. Circle the ONE BEST answer for each.

1. ALL of these are true of Isaiah, son of Amos, EXCEPT:

    a. He lived around 700 B.C.
    b. He was a prophet in the Northern Kingdom.
    c. He was a prophet of doom.
    d. He was a prophet of hope and peace.

2. Isaiah saw the coming destruction as:

    a. Punishment for Israel's sins
    b. Oppression against God's will
    c. A prelude to a holy, peaceful community
    d. a and c

3. Isaiah lived about the time of:
    a. The fall of the Northern Kingdom
    b. The fall of Jerusalem
    c. The exile in Babylon
    d. a and b

4. Isaiah's prophecies included ALL of these EXCEPT:

    a. The coming Messiah
    b. The new beginning for God's people
    c. Syria's defeat of Egypt
    d. Babylon's defeat of Judah

Special Content. Circle the numbers of eleven items which are features of Isaiah Part One.

1. Gifts for the Temple

2. You didn't make me.

3. A stump

4. A time for everything

5. Praise for the Lord

6. The Road of Holiness

7. A wise son

8. The blind will ... see.

9. Satan's power

10. Lord of Armies

11. Living messages

12. The Lord Almighty is determined to do all this.

13. Choose you this day...

14. Holy, holy, holy!

15. The Lord's spirit left him.

16. Drunken leaders and prophets

17. You are the man!

18. No, Lord. Don't send me.

19. Prince of peace.

20. The Lord will destroy death forever.

Check your answers on page 131. Compute your scores on page 136 and enter on the Unit 1 growth record on page 138. Review items you may have missed. Then begin the study of Isaiah Part Two, page 11.

SECTION TEST 2: ISAIAH PART TWO

A. STRUCTURE

Complete the following outline of Isaiah 40--55.

1. Part Two: _____ for the _____

2. _____: _____ _____

3. _____ of _____

4. _____: _____

   and _____

↓

B. NARRATIVE

Persons and Places. Write the number of the person or place before the term with which it is most closely associated.

1. Jerusalem
2. Babylon
3. Exiles
4. The Lord
5. Cyrus
6. Prophet
7. Obedient servant
8. Suffering servant

____ Will bring the people home

____ Given power to conquer nations

____ Told to proclaim the Lord's coming

____ Thought it was God

____ Died for the people's sins

____ Told to prepare a road for the Lord

____ Freed by Cyrus

____ Accepts beatings and insults

C. PROPHECY

Circle the letter of the ONE BEST answer for each:

1. Because the Lord created his people to bring him glory, he will:

   a. Bring them home to Zion
   b. Let them punish the Babylonians
   c. Establish them in new lands
   d. a and b

2. In Part Two are found ALL of the following prophecies EXCEPT:

   a. The Lord is coming to rule with power.
   b. Judah will attack Israel.
   c. Cyrus will rebuild Jerusalem.
   d. Babylon will be destroyed.

3. The servant songs include ALL of these EXCEPT:

   a. The suffering servant
   b. The obedient servant
   c. The reluctant servant
   d. The faithless servant

4. The Lord gave his servant power to:

   a. Make a covenant with all people
   b. See that justice is done on earth
   c. Gain power over other nations
   d. a and b

5. The prophet said the Lord would bring his people back because:

   a. They stopped sinning.
   b. Isaiah prayed for them.
   c. The Lord created them to bring him glory.
   d. They returned to Jerusalem to serve him.

D. FEATURES

Background. Complete these statements.

1. Part Two describes the time of the _____.

2. Christians see Jesus prophesied in the passage about the _____ _____.

3. The purpose of Part Two is to _____ a despairing people, and to show that God is still _____ in _____.

Quotations. Circle the numbers of five quotations from Part Two.

1. Comfort my people.
2. Holy, holy, holy! The Lord Almighty is holy.
3. No matter how much you listen ...
4. The Word of our Lord endures forever.
5. Because of our sins he was wounded.
6. Will have a son and will name him Immanuel
7. Prepare in the wilderness a road for the Lord!
8. A child is born to us! A son is given!
9. A song of my friend and the vineyard
10. Come, everyone who is thirsty.

Check your answers on page 131. Compute your scores on page 136 and enter them on the growth record for Unit 1 on page 138. Review any items missed, and then begin the study of Isaiah Part Three, page 31.

SECTION TEST 3: ISAIAH PART THREE

A. STRUCTURE

Outline. Complete the following outline of Isaiah.

1. Part Three: _____ the _____
   of those who _____

2. I. _____ and _____

3. II. _____ _____

4. III. _____ _____
      and _____

Sequence. Write I, II, or III before each term to show in which section of the outline it is found.

____ Help for the poor and weak-hearted

____ The new creation

____ Two new groups to be welcomed by the Lord to worship in Jerusalem

↓

C. PROPHECY

Circle the number of the ONE BEST answer for each.

1. The Lord wants his people to fast by:

   a. Ending injustice
   b. Sharing their food
   c. Eating no food on holy days
   d. a and b

2. The Lord fills the prophet with his spirit to help:

   a. The lost in the house of Israel
   b. The poor and broken-hearted
   c. Captives and prisoners
   d. b and c

3. The Lord did not answer the people's prayers because:

   a. They did not rebuild the Temple.
   b. They did not pray.
   c. They consulted spirits of the dead.
   d. They ate pork.

4. The people pray for ALL of these reasons EXCEPT:

   a. They are doing good things for the Lord.
   b. God is their father.
   c. God is like the potter, they the clay.
   d. They know they have done wrong.

D. FEATURES

Background. Complete the following statements.

1. Part Three describes the time of the
   _____ of the _____.

2. Part Three was written to _____
   the people and give them direction in
   reestablishing the _____ and
   _____ life of the covenant
   community.

Quotations. Circle the numbers of seven quotations that distinguish Part Three from Parts One and Two.

1. It is your sins that separate you from God when you try to worship him.

2. The Sovereign Lord has filled me with his spirit.

3. Comfort my people.

4. Because of our sins he was wounded.

5. But you are our father, Lord.

6. Holy, holy, holy!

7. Happily Married

8. My Temple will be a house of prayer for all nations.

9. The City That God Loves

10. Prepare in the wilderness a road for the Lord.

11. Share your food with the hungry.

12. Come, everyone who is thirsty.

13. I created them to bring me glory.

14. You said to yourself, "I am God...."

Check answers on page 131. Compute your scores on page 136 and enter them on the Unit 1 growth record on page 138. Review any items missed; then begin the study of Jeremiah on page 11.

SECTION TEST 4: JEREMIAH 1--25

A. STRUCTURE

Outline. Complete the following outline of Jeremiah 1--25.

1. _____'s _____
2. _____ During the _____
   of _____'s _____ _____ _____

Sequence. Number these events from 1-3 in the order in which they are found in Jeremiah.

____ Men of Anathoth plot Jeremiah's death.

____ Jeremiah preaches sermon in the Temple.

____ Jeremiah protests his commission as a prophet because of his youth.

B. NARRATIVE

Write the number of the person or place before the ONE term with which it is most closely associated.

1. Temple
2. Jeremiah
3. Jerusalem
4. Hinnom Valley
5. Priests

____ Place of human sacrifice

____ Complained of curse for obeying God

____ Called a hiding place for robbers

____ Would be attacked and destroyed

____ Watched the breaking of the clay jar

C. PROPHECY

About Prophecies. Circle the ONE BEST answer.

1. The Lord says his people will be punished by:
   a. Their evil
   b. Seventy years of exile
   c. Their prophets
   d. a and b

2. The Lord said ALL of these through Jeremiah EXCEPT:
   a. Judah must confess her guilt.
   b. The Temple will not keep the people safe.
   c. Judah is not as rebellious as Israel.
   d. Israel's God is alive and eternal.

3. The false prophets of Judah:
   a. Were rejected by the people
   b. Proclaimed peace for Jerusalem soon
   c. Worked with Jeremiah
   d. Proclaimed punishment for Babylon in 70 years

4. God's prophecies of doom and promises of blessing:
   a. Can be changed by our way of living
   b. Cannot be changed
   c. Will be carried out within a time span
   d. Have always been carried out

Signs. Write the number of the sign before the ONE term with which it is most closely associated.

1. Almond branch
2. Boiling pot
3. Ruined shorts
4. Potter, clay
5. Tree by stream
6. Baskets of figs

____ Israel is shaped by the Lord's hands.

____ He trusts God.

____ Destruction will come from the north on all who live in this land.

____ God would spoil the pride of his people.

____ The Lord is watching.

____ Exiles to return from Babylon; those in Judah to die.

D. FEATURES

Background. Complete these statements.

1. Jeremiah prophesies mainly about the coming _____.

2. Jeremiah prophesied around ____ hundred B.C.

Quotations. Circle the numbers of three quotations from Jeremiah. (The others are from Isaiah.)

1. They ... fight against you, but ... not defeat you.

2. Comfort my people.

3. Your own evil will punish you.

4. Change the way you are living.

5. Because of your sins he was wounded.

6. Holy, holy, holy! The Lord Almighty is holy!

Check your answers, page 131. Compute your scores, page 136, and enter them on the Unit 1 growth record on page 138. Review any items missed and then begin the study of Jeremiah 26--52 on page 35.

SECTION TEST 5: JEREMIAH 26--52 AND LAMENTATIONS

A. STRUCTURE

<u>Outline</u>. Complete this outline of Jeremiah 26--52 and the statement about Lamentations.

1. _____ in _____'s _____

2. _____ Against the _____

3. The _____ of _____

4. Lamentations is composed of _____ songs.

<u>Sequence</u>. Number these events from 1-4 in the order in which they occurred in Jeremiah.

____ Jeremiah wrote to the exiles in Babylon.

____ Jeremiah was forced to go to Egypt.

____ Jeremiah was freed from prison by Nebuchadnezzar.

____ Jeremiah bought property in Benjamin.

B. NARRATIVE

<u>Persons and Places</u>. Write the number of the person or place before the ONE term with which it is most closely associated.

1. Johanan
2. Jehoiachin
3. Jehoiakim
4. Babylon
5. Egypt
6. Baruch
7. Anathoth
8. Zedekiah
9. Nebuchadnezzar
10. Ebedmelech

____ Led Jerusalem in deceitful covenant

____ Freed after 37 years in prison

____ Defeated at Carchemish

____ Cut and burned the scroll

____ God's instrument of judgment

____ Took Jeremiah to Egypt

____ Recorded Jeremiah's prophecies

____ Rescued Jeremiah from the well

____ Jehoiachin honored above many kings

____ Men wanted to kill Jeremiah

<u>Events</u>. Circle the letter of the ONE BEST answer.

1. ALL of these are true of Jeremiah's trial EXCEPT:

   a. Priests and prophets accused him of treason.
   b. Jeremiah prophesied God would free him.
   c. The elders recalled Micah's prophecy.
   d. Jeremiah's life was spared.

2. Jeremiah wrote ALL of these to the exiles EXCEPT:

   a. Work for the good of the cities you live in.
   b. Pray for these Babylonian cities.
   c. Listen to the prophets there.
   d. Build homes there.

3. Jeremiah was arrested and imprisoned when he:

   a. Prophesied in the palace
   b. Tried to go to his property
   c. Contradicted the court prophets
   d. Prophesied defeat for Zedekiah

4. Jeremiah was thrown into a dry well to die by:

   a. Ebedmelech
   b. Soldiers at Nebuchadnezzar's command
   c. False prophets whose jobs Jeremiah's prophecies had threatened
   d. Johanan

5. ALL of these are true of Jeremiah's scroll EXCEPT:

   a. Jeremiah read it in the Temple.
   b. Baruch recorded Jeremiah's prophecies on it.
   c. Jehudi read it to the officials.
   d. The king listened to it.

6. Johanan's group said they would go to Egypt because:

   a. Jeremiah said they should serve God there.
   b. Jehudi was forcing them to go.
   c. They thought Jeremiah was lying.
   d. The Lord had commanded them.

7. When Baruch gave up, the Lord told him:

   a. I will raise you up to a position of power.
   b. Have faith and you will not suffer.
   c. You will at least escape with your life.
   d. I will preserve that which I have built.

8. When the Babylonians destroyed Jerusalem, they:

   a. Killed the Temple and court officers
   b. Took the Temple treasures away
   c. Killed all they did not take to Babylonia
   d. a and b

9. ALL of these are true of the sorrowing prophet and people EXCEPT:

   a. They continued to suffer attack by the army.
   b. They accepted and approved God's judgment.
   c. They had hope because they knew that the Lord's love is unfailing.
   d. Some starving mothers ate their own children.

C. PROPHECY

<u>Signs</u>. Write the number of the sign before the ONE term that is most closely associated with it.

1. Widow
2. Yoke
3. Book tied to rock
4. Stones in Tahpanhes

____ God would send Nebuchadnezzar to defeat Egypt.

____ Sorrowing Jerusalem after the fall

____ Babylonia would sink and never rise again.

____ Servitude to Babylon in which the Lord was placing nations

About Prophecies. Circle the letter of the ONE BEST answer for each.

1. ALL of these may be considered prophecies of the Messiah EXCEPT:

   a. I will remove their chains.
   b. God's people will be carried off to Babylon.
   c. A new covenant
   d. The Lord Our Salvation

2. Jeremiah saw ALL these fulfilled EXCEPT:

   a. Babylon will destroy Jerusalem.
   b. God will spoil the pride of his people.
   c. Hananiah will die.
   d. The exiles will return to Jerusalem.

3. Those who resisted the Babylonians would:

   a. Be punished by the Lord
   b. Save their lives if they surrendered
   c. Lose their lives but save their souls
   d. a and b

4. Jeremiah said that, after the exile, the people would do ALL of these EXCEPT:

   a. Restore the Box to the Temple
   b. Have God's help in building them up
   c. Have their own land and food
   d. Have seen Babylon defeated

5. The people of Ammon were punished because:

   a. They rejected Milcom.
   b. They trusted in their own power.
   c. God's prophets were stoned there.
   d. None of them worshiped in Jerusalem.

6. Edom was deceived by:

   a. False prophets
   b. The Egyptians
   c. Her own pride
   d. a and b

7. Jeremiah prophesied the Lord's judgment of:

   a. Elam, Philistia, Damascus, Kedar
   b. All people who eat forbidden meat
   c. Damascus, Crete, Arabia, Phoenicia
   d. The Babylonian allies

D. FEATURES

Background. Complete the following statements.

1. The theme of Jeremiah's prophecies is: _____ that can be _____ by _____.

2. Lamentations is sung at the _____

3. of the _____ of _____.

4. The major themes of Lamentations are awareness of _____ and

5. _____ of God's judgment.

Quotations. Write J for Jeremiah or L for Lamentations before seven of the following quotations to distinguish them from those of Isaiah.

1. ____ Babylon will sink, never to rise again.

2. ____ The Lord is just for I have disobeyed him.

3. ____ God is with us!

4. ____ They will serve strangers in a land that is not theirs.

5. ____ Filled with his spirit to bring good news

6. ____ Her enemies succeeded. They hold her in their power.

7. ____ Because of our sins he was wounded.

8. ____ Prince of Peace

9. ____ The Lord has made her suffer for her many sins.

10. ____ I will put my law within them.

11. ____ Prepare in the wilderness a road for the Lord.

12. ____ Build houses and settle down.

Check answers, page 132. Compute your scores, page 136, and enter on the Unit 1 growth record, page 138. After studying any items missed and reviewing outlines and section charts, take Unit Test 1 below.

UNIT TEST 1: ISAIAH, JEREMIAH, AND LAMENTATIONS

A. STRUCTURE

Outline. Complete the outlines and statement (#9).

ISAIAH

1. Part One: The _____ _____

2. Part Two: _____ for the _____

3. Part Three: _____ the _____ of Those Who _____

JEREMIAH

4. _____'s _____

5. _____ During the _____ of _____'s _____ _____ _____

6. _____ in _____ _____

7. _____ Against the _____

8. The _____ of _____

9. Lamentations is composed of _____ songs.

Sequence. Number the events in each group in order.

Number from 1-6:

____ Zedekiah made false covenant to free slaves.
____ Sennacherib withdrew from Jerusalem.
____ Isaiah was called to be a prophet.
____ Hezekiah showed Babylonians his military equipment.
____ Jehoiachin was exiled.
____ Ahaz feared attack by Syria and Israel.

Number from 7-11:

____ The returned Jews rebuilt Jerusalem.
____ Jeremiah prophesied in Egypt.
____ Nebuchadnezzar captured Jerusalem a second time.
____ Cyrus freed the exiles.
____ Babylonian forces withdrew as the Egyptians advanced.

B. NARRATIVE

Persons and Places. Write the number of the person or place before the ONE term with which is is most closely associated.

1. Ahaz
2. Cyrus
3. Baruch
4. Johanan
5. Hezekiah
6. Jeremiah
7. Hananiah
8. Sennacherib
9. Nebuchadnezzar
10. Zedekiah

____ Saw his sons executed and was blinded
____ He was safe, but his descendants would be exiled.
____ Discouraged scribe given God's promise
____ Army commander took Jeremiah to Egypt.
____ False prophet broke Jeremiah's yoke.
____ Rejected Isaiah's message of enemies' defeat out of fear
____ Angel killed soldiers, so he gave up siege.
____ Conquered Babylon and obeyed the Lord
____ Suffered from depression and loneliness
____ God's instrument of judgment

Persons and Places (continued).

11. Assyria
12. Babylon
13. Israel
14. Egypt
15. Syria
16. Temple
17. Jerusalem
18. Carchemish
19. Hinnom Valley
20. Anathoth

____ The Jews thought it would keep them safe.
____ Joined Israel in attacking Judah
____ Men plotted death for Jeremiah.
____ Egypt defeated by Babylon
____ Place of exile for people of Judah
____ Adjacent kingdom feared by Ahaz
____ Conquered cities of Judah but not Jerusalem
____ Jeremiah and Baruch were exiled there.
____ Human sacrifice
____ Destroyed in 587 or 586 B.C.

Events. Circle the letter of the ONE BEST answer.

1. People were shocked at Jeremiah's Temple sermon because of ALL these reasons EXCEPT:

   a. He said God would treat the Temple as he had Shiloh.
   b. They had God's promise of protection.
   c. The Temple was not important to them.
   d. They thought no obedience was required.

2. ALL of these were plots against Jeremiah EXCEPT:

   a. Men from Anathoth wanted to kill Jeremiah.
   b. People broke a jar before the prophet.
   c. Officials threw Jeremiah in a dry well.
   d. People would bring charges against him.

3. Jeremiah wrote ALL of these to the exiles EXCEPT:

   a. The rulers there will not deceive you.
   b. Pray for the Babylonians with whom you live.
   c. Work for the Babylonian cities.
   d. Plant gardens and eat what you grow.

4. Jeremiah bought a field in Anathoth:

   a. Because he was the closest of kin
   b. And tried to see it as enemies retreated
   c. And was arrested for desertion
   d. a, b, and c

5. Jeremiah's scroll of prophecies was:

   a. Recorded by Baruch
   b. Read by Jeremiah in the Temple
   c. Cut and burned by Jehoiakim
   d. a and c

C. PROPHECY

Signs. Write the number of the sign before the ONE meaning of that sign in each group.

1. Baskets of figs
2. Naked prophet
3. A child is born
4. Immanuel
5. Almond branch
6. The Lord's banquet
7. Boiling pot
8. Stump

____ Northern enemy will destroy Judah.
____ Exiles will return, but Jews in Judah and Egypt will die.
____ Foolish to trust Egypt and Syria for help
____ Israel and Syria will not take Jerusalem.
____ David's descendant to be the new king
____ God watching to see that his word is carried out
____ God will destroy death.
____ David's successor will rule to the end.

Signs (continued).

9. Ruined shorts
10. Desert bush
11. Tree by stream
12. Potter, clay
13. Ox yoke
14. Stones in Tahpanhes
15. Widow

____ Person who trusts God
____ Jerusalem in sorrow after ruin
____ God will spoil his people's pride.
____ Person who turns away from God
____ The Lord will bring Nebuchadnezzar to defeat Egypt.
____ God placing nations under servitude to Babylon
____ The Lord will not bless the disobedient nor destroy the repentant.

About Prophecies. Circle the letter of the ONE BEST answer for each prophecy.

1. Isaiah: ALL of these were Judah's sins EXCEPT:

    a. Alcoholism
    b. Fear of attack
    c. Imprisoning Isaiah
    d. Celebrating under siege

2. In Isaiah the Lord promised to:

    a. Give his people joy
    b. Show his people a great light
    c. Relieve their burdens
    d. a, b, and c

3. In Part Two, Isaiah prophesied:

    a. God will bring his people home.
    b. Jerusalem will be destroyed.
    c. The Box will be restored to the Temple.
    d. a and b

4. The Lord's servant was ALL of these EXCEPT:

    a. Killed
    b. The means of the people's forgiveness
    c. Attacked by the Lord of Armies
    d. God's means of succeeding in his purpose

5. Isaiah says that the poor and the captives will be helped because:

    a. The Lord filled the prophet with his spirit.
    b. The king of Judah restored them.
    c. The Babylonians left them alone.
    d. The High Priest prayed for them.

6. Jeremiah did NOT prophesy that David's descendant:

    a. Would rule wisely
    b. Would protect Jerusalem from attack by enemies
    c. Would be called "The Lord Our Salvation"
    d. Would be the king of Judah

7. Jeremiah did not see this prediction come true:

    a. The people of Judah will serve foreigners.
    b. Jerusalem will be destroyed.
    c. Hananiah will be punished by death.
    d. God will bring his people back.

8. God did NOT want his people to:

    a. Listen humbly to their God
    b. Protect his Temple from the foreign army
    c. Worship him sincerely
    d. Go to Babylon as captives

9. God's people will know joy and peace when:

    a. They build houses in Babylon
    b. The king of Judah is freed
    c. Nebuchadnezzar releases Jeremiah
    d. They return to Jerusalem

10. God will bless the world through:

    a. Babylon and Persia
    b. Egypt, Assyria, and Israel
    c. Israel and Egypt
    d. Judah, Israel, and Syria

D. FEATURES

Background. Complete the following statements.

1. Isaiah saw the coming _____ of Israel.

2. Part Two of Isaiah is known for its beautiful _____ and its

3. prophecies of the _____.

4. Part Three of Isaiah was written to people who had _____ to _____.

5. Jeremiah records both his prophecies and his _____ _____.

6. The theme of Jeremiah's prophecies is _____ that can be

7. _____ by repentance.

8. The major themes of Lamentations are awareness of _____ and

9. _____ of God's _____.

Before each item or quotation write 1, 2, or 3 for Isaiah; J for Jeremiah, or L for Lamentations.

Special Content.

____ Road of Holiness
____ Song of the Vineyard
____ Suffering servant
____ Prince of Peace
____ New exodus
____ New covenant
____ Broken jar
____ Great sorrow (major theme)

Quotations.

____ Prepare in the wilderness a road for the Lord!
____ Change the way you are living.
____ Holy, holy, holy!
____ Come, everyone who is thirsty.
____ The Lord is just, for I have disobeyed him.
____ They will serve strangers in a land that is not theirs.
____ To bring good news to the poor, to heal ...
____ There will always be a descendant of David to rule Israel.
____ The Sovereign Lord will destroy death forever!
____ Because of our sins, he was wounded.
____ Enemies succeeded; they hold her in their power.
____ God is with us!
____ Comfort my people.

Check your answers on page 132. Compute your scores, page 136, and enter them on the Unit 1 growth record, page 138. Check the references for any items missed and then begin the study of Unit 2 on page 56.

UNIT 2: EZEKIEL AND DANIEL

OBJECTIVES

In Unit 2, as in Unit 1, items you are to learn have been classified in four categories: structure, narrative, prophecy, and
features. These are defined on page 5.

Upon completion of Unit 2 you will be able to do at least 90% of
the following:

1. Give the major outline headings of the books of Ezekiel
   and Daniel.

2. Place 5 or 6 events in order in Ezekiel and also in Daniel.

3. Associate 8 persons mentioned in these two books with a name or role.

4. Identify 16 aspects of events or dreams in these books.

5. Associate 20 signs with their meanings, persons, or other related facts.

6. Associate 10 visions with their meanings or other related facts.

7. Identify 21 aspects of 15 prophecies in these books.

8. Distinguish among 13 background facts as true of either Ezekiel, Daniel, or both.

9. Distinguish among 12 quotations and other special items as true of Ezekiel, Daniel, or both.

INSTRUCTIONS

Each page of guided reading in Unit 2 is divided by asterisks into three "frames." DO NOT READ ALL THE
WAY DOWN THE PAGE, but turn the page after reading a single frame. Proceed as follows:

1. Take the Unit 2 pre-test and record your score.
   On this and all tests wording may usually vary
   if the meaning is the same.

2. Study the introduction and outline as you begin
   each book.

3. Note the number and heading of each frame.

4. Read the questions in each frame first.

5. Read the Bible passages assigned. When asked
   to scan a passage, you may skip it, skim over
   it, or read it.

6. Try to answer the questions from memory. Just
   say the answers to yourself. You may write
   them if you wish, but it will double the time
   required.

7. When in doubt, look at the Bible to finish
   answering questions.

8. Then and ONLY THEN turn the page to check your
   answers. Exact wording does not usually matter.

9. Note the drawings to help remember major
   points.

10. Do the Just for Funs if you enjoy them and
    have time. Be sure to follow the instruc-
    tions at the end of the frame even if you
    skip them.

11. Use section charts plus outlines to review
    the structure and major themes of each book.

12. Take section tests as instructed; check
    answers and record your scores in the back
    of this book. Then return to page 61 to
    begin guided reading for the next biblical
    book.

13. Take the unit test. Check answers and record
    your scores on the growth record.

14. As you check unit test answers, look up the
    references for any questions you miss.

15. Complete the Unit 2 growth record on page 138
    and figure your growth in knowledge of the
    content of Ezekiel and Daniel.

Now begin the pre-test for Unit 2 on the next page.

A. STRUCTURE

Outline. Circle the ONE BEST answer for each.

1. The first half of Ezekiel takes place:

   a. Before the fall of Jerusalem
   b. Before the exile
   c. After the fall of Jerusalem
   d. As the exiles return

2. The second major division heading is:

   a. Ezekiel's call
   b. After the fall of Jerusalem
   c. Prophecies of glory
   d. Judgment of nations

3. The third major division heading is:

   a. As the exiles return
   b. After the fall of Jerusalem
   c. The imprisonment of the prophet
   d. The longing of the exiles

4. The first half of Daniel can be called:

   a. The struggle for freedom
   b. Stories about Daniel and his friends
   c. Daniel tells about the end-time
   d. False prophets

5. The second half of Daniel can be titled:

   a. Daniel's rise to power
   b. Conflicts with false prophets
   c. Visions of Daniel
   d. God's love for his people

Sequence. Number these events from 1-6 for Ezekiel and 1-5 for Daniel in the order of their occurrence in these two books.

Ezekiel

____ The prophet's wife dies.

____ Ezekiel hears that Jerusalem has fallen.

____ Ezekiel is exiled to Babylon.

____ Ezekiel is told his tongue will be paralyzed.

____ Ezekiel can talk again.

____ God calls Ezekiel in a vision.

Daniel

____ A king is not allowed to rule for seven years.

____ Daniel is trained for court service.

____ A king makes Daniel third in command.

____ Daniel's friends are faithful when faced with death by burning.

____ Daniel goes into exile.

B. NARRATIVE

Persons. Write the number of the person before the ONE term most closely associated with that person.

1. Ezekiel   ____ Babylonian official
2. Daniel   ____ Shadrach
3. Hananiah   ____ Israel's guardian angel
4. Mishael   ____ King
5. Azariah   ____ Abednego
6. Ashpenaz   ____ Priest
7. Belshazzar   ____ Meshach
8. Michael   ____ Belteshazzar

Events. Circle the letter of the ONE BEST answer.

1. Ezekiel did NOT:

   a. Come to Babylon with Jehoiachin
   b. Become one of the king's advisers
   c. Prophesy to the people of Jerusalem
   d. Prophesy to the exiles in Babylon

2. When the king ordered Daniel's death, Daniel:

   a. Asked for more time to interpret the dream
   b. Prayed that God would reveal the dream
   c. Fasted for two days and nights
   d. a and b

3. Shadrach, Meshach, and Abednego were thrown into the furnace for:

   a. Using the king's cup
   b. Refusing to worship a statue
   c. Praying three times a day
   d. Refusing to bow down to the king

4. Daniel did NOT tell Nebuchadnezzar that the king would:

   a. Die in seven years
   b. Live in exile seven years
   c. Admit that God controls human kingdoms
   d. Live among wild animals

5. The writing on the wall did NOT mean that:

   a. Belshazzar's rule would soon be ended
   b. The king's worth had been measured
   c. The king's son would be killed
   d. The kingdom would be divided

6. Daniel was put in the pit of lions because:

   a. Daniel's enemies had planned his death
   b. He prayed three times a day
   c. Darius had prohibited all requests except those made of him
   d. a, b, and c

C. PROPHECY

<u>Signs</u>. Write the number of the sign before the ONE term with which it is most closely associated.

1. Whitewashed wall
2. No mourning for the wife who died
3. Scratches on a brick
4. Hair cut and burned
5. Climbing through a hole in a wall
6. Oholah and Oholibah
7. Corroded pot
8. Refining furnace
9. The Lord's sword
10. The cedar

____ Idolatrous Samaria and Judah

____ God's restoration of Israel

____ Three stages of judgment throughout Israel

____ The king of Babylon

____ Suffering with no time for grief

____ Sinful Jerusalem needing cleansing

____ God's anger

____ Saying all is well when it is not

____ Refugees from Jerusalem after its fall

____ Siege of Jerusalem

<u>Signs</u> (continued).

11. Crocodile
12. Royal food refused
13. Daniel in lion's pit
14. Blazing furnace
15. Belshazzar's banquet
16. The watchman
17. Corroded pot
18. Gold head, clay feet
19. Chained stump
20. Beautiful prostitute

____ Three Jews choose death over idolatry.

____ A great emperor suffers from mental disorder.

____ God's revelation of a dream and its meaning

____ Offering gifts to pagan nations and idols

____ Daniel broke the king's rule by praying.

____ Responsibility for warning evil persons

____ The king of Egypt

____ Jerusalem needing cleansing from sin

____ Following dietary laws made Jews stronger.

____ Temple cups and bowls were profaned.

<u>Visions</u>. Write the number of the vision before the ONE term with which it is most closely associated.

1. The four beasts
2. The valley of bones
3. Stream flowing from the Temple
4. Angel by the river
5. The Lord-Is-Here
6. Mark on forehead
7. Dazzling light
8. Four creatures flying
9. Seventy years
10. The ram and the goat

____ God's glory leaving Jerusalem

____ Syrian king destroyed without human power

____ Those in God's book to enjoy life

____ Jerusalem's restoration in 490 years

____ Life wherever it goes

____ Those disturbed at Jerusalem's sin

____ New life for a dead Israel

____ New Jerusalem in the end-time

____ God's presence

____ Eternal royal power for God's people

<u>About Prophecies</u>. Circle the ONE BEST answer.

1. The vision of the new Temple does NOT include:

    a. A stream flowing straight to the Temple
    b. Trees bearing fruit each month
    c. Leaves of the trees with healing power
    d. Levites excluded from the Most Holy Place

2. An evil man who stops sinning will

    a. Still be punished by death
    b. Have his punishment reduced
    c. Live
    d. Teach others

3. Egyptians will find the ungodly of other nations:

    a. Have been taking over their nation
    b. Will be punished with famines
    c. A warning to Egypt
    d. In the world of the dead

4. Concerning the king of Judah's treaty with Babylon, ALL of these are true EXCEPT:

    a. The treaty kept Judah quiet and docile.
    b. The king broke the treaty.
    c. The king sent to Egypt for an army.
    d. The king of Syria would occupy Judah.

5. The Lord's presence returned to the Temple when:

    a. The dazzling light appeared.
    b. The man shining like bronze entered the Most Holy Place.
    c. The figure on the throne spoke.
    d. All the people confessed their sins.

Write the number of each prophecy before the ONE term with which it is most closely associated.

6. New covenant

7. Dazzling light moved above the creatures

8. Sour grapes

9. Promised to exiles

10. Tyre's punishment

11. Gog and his men were punished

12. Measuring the Temple

13. Attack on Jerusalem

14. The good shepherd

15. Final vision of the future

____ Celebrating Jerusalem's fall

____ Prophet "taken" to the Temple

____ Return to Judah

____ Man shining like bronze

____ God's presence leaving the Temple

____ The Lord taking care of his people

____ Gog of Magog

____ Obedient hearts

____ A severe earthquake in Israel

____ Responsibility for one's own sins

D. FEATURES

Write E for Ezekiel and D for Daniel before each background fact or special item.

Background.

____ Strongly influenced post-exilic Judaism

____ Sees God as Lord of world history

____ Came to Babylon as captive with Jehoiachin

____ Found among the Writings of the Jewish canon

____ Most contemporary scholars date the writing in the time of the Maccabees.

____ Known as an apocalyptic writing

____ A new covenant for the future

____ Prophecies before the capture of Jerusalem

____ Half of the book was written in Aramaic.

____ Part of the book is addressed to the people of Jerusalem.

____ Doom for Jerusalem and judgment of nations

____ Stressed the individual's responsibility for his own sin

Special Content. One item is both E and D.

____ Can these bones come back to life?

____ God's chosen leader will be killed unjustly.

____ There is no other god who can rescue like this.

____ Mortal man (Son of man)

____ You did not honor the God who determines whether you live or die.

____ On the throne was a figure that looked like a man.

____ I heard the Lord speak .... I felt his power.

____ Their royal power will never end.

____ Wherever it flows, it will bring life.

____ The angels Michael and Gabriel

____ He had not been hurt at all for he trusted God.

____ I do not enjoy seeing a sinner die.

Check your answers on page 133. Compute your scores on page 136 and enter on the Unit 2 growth record, page 138. Then begin the study of Ezekiel on page 61.

EZEKIEL

110 BEFORE THE FALL OF JERUSALEM   (chapters 1--24)

    111 EZEKIEL'S CALL AND FIRST VISION

    112 DOOM FOR JERUSALEM

        112A Warnings of Disaster

        112B Another Vision of God and the Temple

        112C Signs of Coming Judgment

210 JUDGMENT OF NATIONS   (chapters 25--32)

    211 TYRE AND OTHER PALESTINIAN NEIGHBORS

    212 EGYPT

220 AFTER THE FALL OF JERUSALEM   (chapters 33--48)

    221 PROMISE AND HOPE

    222 AGAINST GOG

    223 THE WORSHIPING COMMUNITY RESTORED

        223A The New Temple

        223B God's Return and New Rules

        223C The Surroundings of the Temple

DANIEL

310 STORIES ABOUT DANIEL AND HIS FRIENDS   (chapters 1--6)

    311 ROYAL FOOD REFUSED

    312 NEBUCHADNEZZAR'S DREAM

    313 THE BLAZING FURNACE

    314 NEBUCHADNEZZAR'S MADNESS

    315 BELSHAZZAR'S BANQUET

    316 DANIEL IN THE PIT OF LIONS

320 VISIONS OF DANIEL   (chapters 7--12)

    321 THE FOUR BEASTS

    322 THE RAM AND THE GOAT

    323 THE SEVENTY YEARS

    324 THE ANGEL BY THE TIGRIS RIVER

NOTE: *You are asked to memorize all headings except those with a letter after the numeral. To help you learn the outline for each book, structure drawings are used. Each time a new heading is introduced, the structure is built that far. Outlines move from top to bottom within the structure drawings.*

The book of Ezekiel (sounds like "we SEEK yell") was written during the period just before and just after the fall of Jerusalem in 587/586 B.C.* Many of its prophecies are dated and given in chronological order, unlike those of Jeremiah and other prophetic writings. Along with Jehoiachin and other educated persons of Jerusalem, Ezekiel had been exiled to Babylon in 598/597 B.C.* He prophesied both in Babylon and in Jerusalem.

Most of Ezekiel is a message of doom for Jerusalem and judgment on the nations. His listeners did not repent; in fact, they were not even hostile as they had been to Jeremiah. People enjoyed hearing Ezekiel and they went on their way undisturbed. The last section gives promises of salvation for Israel, including the new Temple in the new Jerusalem, restored to end-time perfection.

Ezekiel's teaching stressed individual responsibility for sin and the need for holiness. He spoke of the same new heart and new covenant as Jeremiah, and Ezekiel's methods of prophesying were even more unusual. He acted out many parables, even refraining from mourning his wife's death until Jerusalem fell, to demonstrate the coming tragedy that was beyond grief. Ezekiel also prophesied by means of visions. His visions of God moving above the creatures and of the new Jerusalem are among those that appear later in the Revelation to John. Ezekiel's writings were influential in the development of post-exilic Judaism.

---

* Different dates are given by different sources. The difference in time is insignificant.

Study the outline of Ezekiel opposite. Then turn to 100 on the next page.

* * * * * * * * * * * * *

300   INTRODUCTION TO DANIEL

The book of Daniel appears in the Jewish canon among the Writings rather than with the Prophets, as in the Christian canon. It is an apocalyptic writing, disclosing hidden things by means of dreams, visions, signs, and symbols. About half of it is written in the Aramaic (sounds like "Sarah MAY lick") language.

It is divided into two parts. Chapters 1--6 are stories about Daniel and his three friends in the service of Nebuchadnezzar of Babylon. This part is written in the third person. The six stories include two dreams of Nebuchadnezzar which Daniel interpreted: the composite metal statue with clay feet and the tall tree chopped down. Chapters 7--12 are written in the first person. They contain four visions of Daniel: the four beasts, the goat and the ram, the seventy weeks, and the angel by the Tigris River.**

The book of Daniel represents a further broadening of Jewish theology. Earlier, Yahweh was thought of as the God of Israel alone, but in Daniel God is clearly the Lord of world history. Daniel expresses complete trust in the God who determines the rise and fall of world empires, who is in complete control of the past, present, and future.

The stories and visions of Daniel are set in the reigns of Nebuchadnezzar, Belshazzar, and Darius the Mede, from 598 to 538 B.C. Traditionally the writing is dated during the time of the exile. For historical and literary reasons, however, most contemporary scholars hold that the book was written during the Maccabean revolt against Antiochus Epiphanes, 167-164 B.C.

** The Greek versions of Daniel include passages not found in the Hebrew-Aramaic Daniel: The Song of Azariah and the Three Young Men (ch. 3), Susanna and the Elder (ch. 13), and Bel and the Dragon (ch. 14). These passages do appear in Catholic versions and in the Apocrypha of many Protestant Bibles today.

Study the outline of Daniel opposite. Then turn to 300 on the next page.

Circle the letter of the ONE BEST answer for each of the following. (Check answers upside down at the end of the frame.)

1. During the period covered by the book of
    Ezekiel, Ezekiel was:
    a. Living in Jerusalem before the fall
    b. Exiled along with Jehoiachin
    c. Exiled after the fall of Jerusalem
    d. Living in Babylonia
    e. b and d

2. Ezekiel prophesied to:
    a. The people of Jerusalem
    b. The exiles in Babylonia
    c. The Babylonians
    d. a and b
    e. a, b, and c

3. Ezekiel's major themes include:
    a. Judgment on the nations
    b. Doom for Jerusalem
    c. Reform of courts
    d. Sorrow for sin and destruction
    e. a and b

4. Ezekiel's teaching stressed:
    a. Individual responsibility for sin
    b. Keeping the Sabbath day holy
    c. Justice for the poor and oppressed
    d. Israel's mission
    e. c and d

5. Ezekiel did NOT make use of:
    a. Visions
    b. Signs
    c. Interpreted dreams
    d. Acted parables
    e. Descriptions of the end-time

6. Ezekiel's thought contributed to:
    a. Later Judaism
    b. Individual responsibility for sin
    c. New covenant thinking
    d. a and b
    e. a, b, and c

Begin guided reading at 110 on the next page.

Begin guided reading at 110 on the next page.

Answers: 1. e; 2. d; 3. e; 4. a; 5. c; 6. e

* * * * * * * * * * * * * *

Circle the letter of the ONE BEST answer for each of the following statements. (Check answers upside down at the end of the frame.)

1. Daniel was ALL of the following EXCEPT:
    a. Listed with the Writings in the Jewish
        canon
    b. Placed among the Historical Books in the
        Catholic canon
    c. Placed among the Prophets in the Protestant
        canon
    d. An example of apocalyptic writing
    e. a and d

2. ALL of the following are true of the book of
    Daniel EXCEPT:
    a. It contains four visions.
    b. It discloses hidden things through signs
        and visions.
    c. About half the stories are set in the time
        of Darius the Mede.
    d. About half the book is written in Aramaic.
    e. About half the book is written in the first
        person.

3. The debate about the date of writing has been
    between these two times:
    a. The exile and the Maccabees
    b. The rebuilding and Roman rule
    c. The 5th and 1st centuries
    d. The 6th and 2nd centuries
    e. a and d

4. The major contribution of Daniel to theological
    thought is:
    a. A change from a narrow to a world view of
        God
    b. The importance of visions
    c. Scholarship to date original writing
    d. Writing in the language of the people
    e. Shedding light on a period that has few
        written records

Continue guided reading at 310 on the next page.

Continue guided reading at 310 on the next page.

Answers: 1. b; 2. c; 3. e; 4. a

110   BEFORE THE FALL OF JERUSALEM (chapters 1--24)

NOTE: Jerusalem fell in 587 or 586 B.C.

111   EZEKIEL'S CALL AND FIRST VISION

Read Ezekiel 1--3.

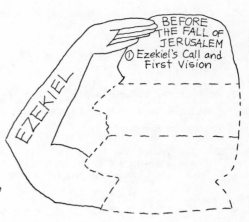

1. When Ezekiel the priest heard the Lord speak and felt his power, he saw a vision of four creatures. What showed the presence of the Lord?

2. The Lord appointed Ezekiel to be a watchman for the nation of Israel. What would be the consequences of Ezekiel's not warning evil sinners and good men who started to sin?

3. What happened to Ezekiel when God's spirit entered him in the valley?

* * * * * * * * * * * *

210   JUDGMENT OF NATIONS (chapters 25--32)

211   TYRE AND OTHER PALESTINEAN NEIGHBORS

Scan Ezekiel 25; read 26; scan 27; read 28.

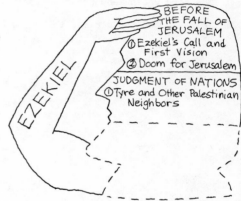

1. What would the Lord do because the people of Tyre were cheering at the fall of Jerusalem, their rival?

2. Why was the Lord going to punish the king of Tyre?

* * * * * * * * * * * *

310   STORIES ABOUT DANIEL AND HIS FRIENDS (chapters 1--6)

311   ROYAL FOOD REFUSED

Read Daniel 1.

NOTE: This story is set in the reign of Nebuchadnezzar of Babylon.
Though it is dated in the third year of Jehoiakim of Judah
(609-598 B.C.), it seems to reflect the first deportation
under Jehoiachin, in 598 B.C. See 2 Kings 24.

1. What were the names given Daniel, Hananiah, Mishael, and Azariah?

2. Why did Daniel and his friends refuse the court food?

3. How did Daniel convince the guard to let them eat vegetables instead?

111

1. The dazzling light that came from the figure on the throne, "that looked like a man."

2. In both cases the men die for their sins and Ezekiel is held responsible.

3. The spirit raised Ezekiel to his feet and said his tongue would be paralyzed so he could not warn the people until God spoke to him again.

NOTE: Throughout the book, Ezekiel is addressed as "mortal man" and addresses God as "Sovereign Lord." Most other English versions translate these as "son of man" and "Lord God."

* * * * * * * * * * * * *

211

1. The Lord would send Nebuchadnezzar to conquer them.

2. He was proud and claimed to be a god.

* * * * * * * * * * * * *

311

1. Daniel - Belteshazzar (sounds like "Mel, the DAZZ-ler")
   Hananiah (like "Stan 'n MY-ra") - named Shadrach (like "SAD rack")
   Mishael (like "WISH-a-well") - named Meshach (like "WEE shack")
   Azariah (like "has a FLY, huh?") - named Abednego (like "a BED to go")

2. They would not eat anything ritually unclean.

3. The guard agreed to a ten-day experiment. At the end, the three Jews looked better and stronger than those who ate the court food.

112   DOOM FOR JERUSALEM

112 A   Warnings of Disaster

Read Ezekiel 4--5; scan 6; read 7.

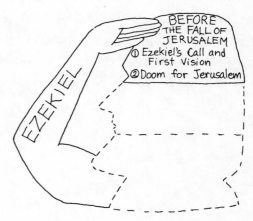

1. When Ezekiel scratched lines on the brick, dug trenches, and set the iron pan between him and the brick, what was he demonstrating?

2. After Ezekiel cut his hair and burned one of the three parts of it, where would the fire spread?

3. What can Israel expect, that the Lord says is coming?

* * * * * * * * * * * *

212   EGYPT

Read Ezekiel 29; scan 30; read 31--32.

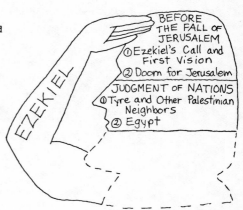

1. What would the Lord do to Israel when Nebuchadnezzar conquered Egypt?

2. The prophet compared Egypt to a beautiful cedar tree. Why did the Lord reject it as it grew taller?

3. What does the Lord say that the king of Egypt is like?

4. Where would the Egyptians find the ungodly from other countries?

* * * * * * * * * * * *

312   NEBUCHADNEZZAR'S DREAM

Read Daniel 2.

NOTE: This story and the next five were written in Aramaic instead of Hebrew.

1. Why didn't the royal advisers interpret the king's dream?

2. When the king ordered the death of all advisers, including Daniel, what two things did Daniel do?

3. What happened when Daniel described the metal statue with clay feet and its meaning concerning future kingdoms?

1. He was enacting the siege of Jerusalem.

2. The **fire** would spread to the whole nation of Israel (the third stage of judgment of Israel's unfaithfulness).

3. The end is coming, the day of disaster.

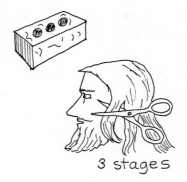

3 stages

* * * * * * * * * * * *

212

1. The Lord would make them strong when Nebuchadnezzar conquered Egypt.

2. It grew proud.

3. A crocodile

4. In the world of the dead

King of Egypt

Check the JUST FOR FUN on the next page and then follow instructions at the end of its answer page.

* * * * * * * * * * * *

312

1. They did not know what he had dreamed, and the king would not **tell** them.

2. Daniel asked for time to tell and interpret the dream himself. He asked his friends to pray to God, asking him to explain the mystery.

3. The king made Daniel head of his advisers and praised Daniel's God.

King's advisors

112B Another Vision of God and the Temple

Read Ezekiel 8--9.

1. From Ezekiel's house in exile, where did God's spirit take him?

2. God was outraged at the idolatry because it was <u>right in the Temple</u>! Can you find the four forms of idolatry practiced there?

3. Who were the only persons not killed by the six men?

* * * * * * * * * * * * * *

JUST FOR FUN!   Ezekiel: I Will Punish!

    "I will punish nations and kings!"   Nations hate Judah: they act so cruelly.

    God is angry--just what bad things   Kings claim God's power--oh, so cooly!

    Have been done, such wrath he brings?   God brings justice--oh, so truly!

Can you name three of the five nations and the two kings (king of ____) who fit these rhymes?

Check your answers on the next page.

* * * * * * * * * * * * * *

313 THE BLAZING FURNACE

Read Daniel 3.

NOTE: This, like the first two stories, is set in the
       time of Nebuchadnezzar.

1. What did Nebuchadnezzar command everyone to do?

2. What happened when Shadrach, Meshach, and Abednego refused?

3. What happened to the three young Jews then?

4. What did Nebuchadnezzar do when he saw that?

112B

1. Grabbing Ezekiel by the hair, the spirit took him to the Temple in Jerusalem.

2. Idol at the North Gate, leaders worshiping images of unclean animals, women weeping over the death of the god Tammuz, men worshiping the sun.

3. Those whose foreheads bore the mark put there by the man in linen to show that they were disturbed by the sin in Jerusalem.

* * * * * * * * * * * * * *

JUST FOR FUN Answers

Nation	Sin	Reference		Kings	Sin	Reference
Ammon	Despised Israel	Ezekiel 25:2,3,6				
Moab	Said Judah was like other nations	Ezekiel 25:8		King of Tyre	Claimed to be a god	Ezekiel 28:2,6
Edom	Took cruel revenge on Judah	Ezekiel 25:12		King of Egypt	Grew proud; claimed to have made the Nile	Ezekiel 31:10; 29:3
Philistia	Took revenge and hated enemies	Ezekiel 25:15				
Egypt	Let Israel down when help was requested	Ezekiel 29:6-7				

Continue with 220 on the next page.

* * * * * * * * * * * * * *

313

1. He commanded everyone to bow down to worship the gold statue that he had made.

2. The three young Jews were thrown into a furnace so hot that those who threw them in were burned up at once.

3. They walked around in the flames unharmed, and a fourth person was seen with them.

4. Praising their God, Nebuchadnezzar released them and gave them important government positions.

112B. Another Vision (*continued*)

Read Ezekiel 10--11.

4. What did the dazzling light of the Lord's presence leave when it moved above the creatures?

5. What did God promise the exiles and what would they then be?

6. In Ezekiel 11:22 the living creatures began to fly with the dazzling light over them. What did God's glory leave then?

PROPHESIED
before and after
the Fall
c. 587 B.C.

* * * * * * * * * * * * *

220 AFTER THE FALL OF JERUSALEM (chapters 33--48)

221 PROMISE AND HOPE

Read Ezekiel 33.

1. When the Lord made Ezekiel the watchman for Israel, for what did he hold Ezekiel responsible?

NOTE: Ezekiel 33:11--"I do not enjoy seeing a sinner die. I would rather see him stop sinning and live"--is often used in Christian worship.

2. When was Ezekiel's speech restored?

EZEKIEL

BEFORE THE FALL OF JERUSALEM
① Ezekiel's Call and First Vision
② Doom for Jerusalem

JUDGMENT OF NATIONS
① Tyre and Other Palestinian Neighbors
② Egypt

AFTER THE FALL OF JERUSALEM
① Promise and Hope

* * * * * * * * * * * * *

314 NEBUCHADNEZZAR'S MADNESS

Read Daniel 4.

1. How did Daniel interpret the dream Nebuchadnezzar had about the tree chopped down with the stump chained?

2. The dream came true. What did Nebuchadnezzar do at the end of the seven years?

STORIES ABOUT DANIEL AND HIS FRIENDS

① Royal Food Refused
② Nebuchadnezzar's Dream
③ The Blazing Furnace
④ Nebuchadnezzar's Madness

4. The dazzling light left the Temple.

5. He would bring them back to Israel and give them obedient hearts and "they will be my people, and I will be their God." (Note this renewal of the covenant.)

6. God's glory left Jerusalem then.

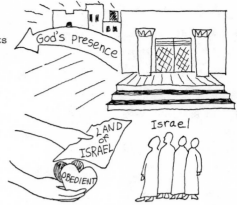

Check the JUST FOR FUN on the next page and follow instructions on its answer page.

* * * * * * * * * * * * * *

221

1. He held Ezekiel responsible for the death of any evil man whom Ezekiel failed to warn to change.

2. When he was told that Jerusalem had fallen

NOTE: The Lord had spoken of paralyzing Ezekiel's tongue and later restoring his speech seven years earlier in Ezekiel 3:26-27. Ezekiel had predicted the fall of Jerusalem three years earlier when his wife died, in 24:15-27.

* * * * * * * * * * * * * *

314

1. Daniel said Nebuchadnezzar was the tree, a great king. Soon he would have to give up his rule. He would have the mind of an animal for seven years and live with wild animals. Then he would return to rule again.

2. Upon receiving his own mind back, he admitted that God controlled all human kingdoms and he praised God.

Ezekiel reports that his two visions of God took exactly the same form. Can you imagine the fantastic images that he describes? On a separate sheet, try your hand at drawing them, giving them an image more complete than that shown in the *Good News Bible*. Ezekiel describes the four creatures "beneath the God of Israel" in chapters 1 and 10—11.

In the Revelation to John, there are also four creatures, but there they each have just one of the four faces that Ezekiel describes as four faces on each creature (Rev. 4:7 and Ez. 1:10 and 10:14).

Turn to the next page for more about these visions.

* * * * * * * * * * * * * *

221 PROMISE AND HOPE (*continued*)

   Read Ezekiel 34; scan 35--36; read 37.

3. The shepherds of Israel used God's sheep instead of tending them.
    Who, then, would be the shepherd of God's people?

4. What vision did the Lord give Ezekiel to show that he would bring
    his people back to life and let them live in their own land?

5. What was represented by two sticks held together end to end?

PROPHESIED
c. 587 B.C.

* * * * * * * * * * * * * *

315 BELSHAZZAR'S BANQUET

   Read Daniel 5.

1. After the royal party drank out of cups taken from the Temple,
    a human hand wrote on the wall. What did Daniel say that meant?

2. What happened to Daniel and to the king?

NOTE: The setting for this story is the reign of "King Belshazzar"
       (sounds like "Mel HAS her"). The historical Belshazzar was
       son of Nabonidus, not Nebuchadnezzar, and crown prince and
       vice-regent, not king. The time would be about 538 B.C.,
       when the Medo-Persian army defeated Babylon.

Ezekiel, the priestly prophet, is regarded by most scholars as the father of post-exilic Judaism, preceding Ezra, who shared this title with him. The exile in Babylon did foster changes in Jewish theology and practice which Ezekiel had the wisdom to recognize. His two visions of God are indicative of such a change.

For centuries the people of the United Kingdom (and later of Judah) had proclaimed the need to worship God in the Temple at Jerusalem. Those in exile could not. Ezekiel's two visions of God, the first in Babylon and the second in Jerusalem, were identical, giving the exiles hope that God was present with them even though they could no longer worship in the Temple. God promised, "I will be present with them in the lands where they have gone" (Ez. 11:16). The informal gatherings to worship and study while still in Babylon were probably forerunners of the later synagogues.

Continue with 112C on the next page.

* * * * * * * * * * * * * *

221

3. The Lord will take care of them as a good shepherd.

4. The valley of dry bones that came to life when Ezekiel prophesied to them that God would do this

5. Israel and Judah reunited

* * * * * * * * * * * * * *

315

1. The days of Belshazzar's kingdom were numbered. He had been weighed and was found wanting. His kingdom would be divided between the Medes and the Persians.

2. Daniel was made third in power. The king was slain as Darius the Mede seized power.

72

112C Signs of Coming Judgment

Read Ezekiel 12--13; scan 14--15.

1. When the prophet escaped through the hole in the wall as a refugee, what did this symbolize?

2. Why would the Lord break down the wall that the prophets had whitewashed, letting it kill them?

* * * * * * * * * * * * * *

222 AGAINST GOG

Read Ezekiel 38.

1. What will Gog, ruler of Meshech and Tubal in the land of Magog, do?

2. What will happen when Gog does that?

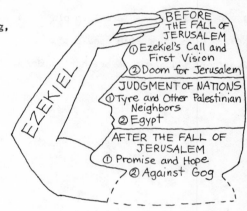

* * * * * * * * * * * * * *

316 DANIEL IN THE PIT OF LIONS

Read Daniel 6.

1. What rule, made by Daniel's enemies and signed by Darius, did Daniel break?

2. What happened to Daniel when he was thrown in the lions' pit?

3. What did Darius do the next morning?

NOTE: This story is set in the reign of Darius the Mede, who is unknown to historians. Cyrus the Persian, king of Medes and Persians, conquered the last king of Babylon. Darius I of Persia came to the throne sixteen years later.

112C

1. It was a message for the prince and people in Jerusalem that they would be refugees and captives.

2. The false prophets assured Jerusalem that all was well when it was not.

NOTE: The King James Version translates it: "Saying 'Peace!' when there is no peace."

* * * * * * * * * * * * * *

222

1. Gog will invade Israel to plunder it.

NOTE: Revelation 20:8 speaks of this.

2. There will be a severe earthquake in Israel and Gog and his men will be punished.

* * * * * * * * * * * * * *

316

1. Darius had ordered the death of anyone who made a request from any god or man except the king for a 30 day period.

2. Daniel was not hurt by the lions, for he had trusted God.

3. Darius released Daniel the next morning and ordered everyone to fear Daniel's God.

Check the JUST FOR FUN on the next page. Then follow instructions at the end of its answer page.

112C   Signs of Coming Judgment *(continued)*

   Read Ezekiel 16--17.

3. When the Lord made Jerusalem famous in every nation for her
    perfect beauty, what did she do?

4. The parable of the eagles and the vine means punishment for
    Judah. What does the parable of the cedar mean?

NOTE: The cedar is Judah's royal family, the house of David
       (Ez 17:3, 12); the sprout on the branch is the Messiah,
       David's descendant (Is. 11:1; Jer. 23:5). Israel's highest
       mountain is Jerusalem or Zion (Is. 2:2; Mic. 4:1).

5. Why will the king of Judah be caught as in a "hunter's net"
    and die in Babylon?

PROPHESIED
to Jews
in Babylon
and
in Jerusalem

* * * * * * * * * * * * * *

222   AGAINST GOG *(continued)*

   Read Ezekiel 39.

3. What will happen in Travelers' Valley?

4. When the Lord brings the people back to the land of Israel, what will he pour out on his people?

* * * * * * * * * * * * * *

JUST FOR FUN!   Daniel in Disguise

Can you recognize an event in Daniel from each of these analagous or related phrases?

1. Carrots, not cake

2. Mind reading demanded

3. With the price of gold out of sight, people were putting their faith in it.

4. The man named "Mob" or "Legion" whom Jesus healed (Mark 5:1-20)

5. The politician had a ghost writer prepare his speeches.

6. Born Free

Turn to the next page for answers.

112C

3. As a prostitute she offered everything the Lord gave her, including her children, to her lovers, the pagan nations and their idols.

4. God will restore Israel, or the house of David, as he said he would.

5. He broke the treaty he had made in God's name. (He sent to Egypt for horses and an army.)

* * * * * * * * * * * * * *

222

3. Gog and his defeated army will be buried there.

4. He will pour out his spirit on his people.

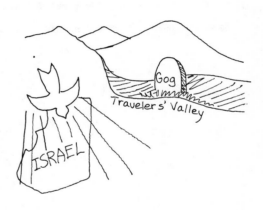

* * * * * * * * * * * * * *

JUST FOR FUN Answers

1. Simple food was preferred to the king's rich forbidden food, much of which had been offered to idols (ch.1).

2. Nebuchadnezzar demanded that his advisers tell him <u>what</u> he had dreamed as well as what it meant (ch.2).

3. The people worshiped the gold statue (ch.3).

4. Daniel told Nebuchadnezzar that he would lose his sanity for seven years, and would live among animals (ch.4).

5. The writing on Belshazzar's wall was written by a hand whose owner people could not see, just as the politician's speeches were written by a writer we cannot see (ch.5).

6. The lions did not hurt Daniel, just as the lion in <u>Born Free</u> did not hurt its owner (ch.6).

Continue with 320 on the next page.

112C Signs of Coming Judgment *(continued)*

Read Ezekiel 18; scan 19; read 20.

6. What was the Lord's will concerning the proverb of sour grapes?

7. What will happen if an evil man stops sinning?

8. The Israelites were rebellious when they were led out of Egypt. When will God accept their sacrifice again?

PROPHESIED just before and just after the Fall of Jerusalem

* * * * * * * * * * * *

223 THE WORSHIPING COMMUNITY RESTORED
223A The New Temple

Read Ezekiel 40:1-6; scan 40:7--42:20.

1. Where was Ezekiel taken in the vision?

2. Ezekiel was told he had been brought there to report what he saw to Israel. What did the man who shone like bronze do to the Temple?

EZEKIEL

BEFORE THE FALL OF JERUSALEM
① Ezekiel's Call and First Vision
② Doom for Jerusalem

JUDGMENT OF NATIONS
① Tyre and Other Palestinian Neighbors
② Egypt

AFTER THE FALL OF JERUSALEM
① Promise and Hope
② Against Gog
③ The Worshiping Community Restored

* * * * * * * * * * * *

320 VISIONS OF DANIEL (chapters 7--12)
321 THE FOUR BEASTS

Read Daniel 7.

NOTE: The setting for this vision is the first year of Belshazzar's reign.

1. What did the four beasts that came out of the sea represent?

2. Daniel saw one who had been living forever ("Ancient of days") give authority to one who looked like a human being ("like a Son of man"). What did that mean?

STORIES ABOUT DANIEL AND HIS FRIENDS

① Royal Food Refused
② Nebuchadnezzar's Dream
③ The Blazing Furnace
④ Nebuchadnezzar's Madness
⑤ Belshazzar's Banquet
⑥ Daniel in the Pit of Lions

VISIONS OF DANIEL

① The Four Beasts

112C

6. It was never to be used again because the person who sins will die, not his son.

NOTE: Jeremiah 31:29 also speaks of sour grapes.

7. He will be forgiven and will live.

8. God will accept them when he brings his people out of foreign countries and back to Israel.

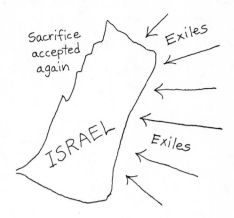

* * * * * * * * * * * * * *

223A

1. First he was taken to a high mountain in Israel. Then the Lord brought him closer to the city and then finally inside the Temple. (Take credit for any part of this answer.)

2. He measured it.

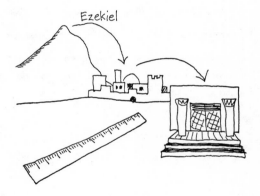

* * * * * * * * * * * * * *

321

1. Four great empires on earth, the four strongest and most oppressive toward God's people

NOTE: This vision is similar to the ones described in Revelation 13 and 17.

2. It meant that God would give his people a king whose authority and royal power will never end.

112C   Signs of Coming Judgment *(continued)*

   Read Ezekiel 21--22.

9.   Whose sword will serve as the sword of the Lord?

10.   What will melt the Israelites the way fire melts ore?

* * * * * * * * * * * * * *

223B   God's Return and New Rules

   Read Ezekiel 43--44; scan 45--46.

1.   When Ezekiel saw the same dazzling light that he had seen when the Lord left the Temple, what happened?

2.   What people will be excluded from the Temple?

3.   What priests will be excluded from the priesthood?

* * * * * * * * * * * * * *

322   THE RAM AND THE GOAT

   Read Daniel 8.

The ram, representing Media Persia, was destroyed by the goat, representing Greece and the four kingdoms into which Alexander's empire was divided. What would happen to the destructive king (Antiochus) who would defy the greatest king of all (God)?

NOTE: The setting for this vision is the third year of Belshazzar's reign. Starting with chapter 8, the rest of the book of Daniel is written in Hebrew.

323   SEVENTY YEARS

   Read Daniel 9.

NOTE: The setting for this vision is the first year of the reign of Darius the Mede.

1.   Daniel prayed for the sins of the people. What did Gabriel tell him that the 70 years in Jeremiah's prophecy really meant?

2.   What would happen to God's chosen leader?

STORIES ABOUT DANIEL AND HIS FRIENDS
① Royal Food Refused
② Nebuchadnezzar's Dream
③ The Blazing Furnace
④ Nebuchadnezzar's Madness
⑤ Belshazzar's Banquet
⑥ Daniel in the Pit of Lions

VISIONS OF DANIEL
① The Four Beasts
② The Ram and the Goat
③ The Seventy Years

112C

9. The sword of the king of Babylon

10. The Lord's anger will melt them like a refining furnace.

* * * * * * * * * * * * * *

223B

1. The Lord returned to the Temple, saying he would live there and rule the people of Israel forever.

2. Uncircumcised foreigners and people who disobey God

3. Levites were to be excluded from serving God as priests and from the Most Holy Place because they had worshiped idols.

* * * * * * * * * * * * * *

322

NOTE: Daniel, like Ezekiel, is addressed as "mortal man."

He would be destroyed without the use of any human power.

323

1. It meant seven times 70 years (70 weeks of years) or 490 years from the command to rebuild Jerusalem till sin will be forgiven, eternal justice established, and the Temple rededicated.

2. He would be killed unjustly.

NOTE: Christians have understood verses 26-27 to be a prediction of the death of Jesus Christ and of the destruction of the Temple in 70 A.D. See Mark 13:14.

112C   Signs of Coming Judgment *(continued)*
   Read Ezekiel 23--24.

11.   Who were Oholah (sounds like "more CO-la") and Oholibah
       (sounds like "aw HO-ly sod!")?

12.   What did the corroded pot represent?

13.   The Lord tells Ezekiel not to mourn when his wife dies. How is
       this a sign to the people of Jerusalem?

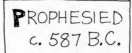

PROPHESIED
c. 587 B.C.

* * * * * * * * * * * * * *

223C   The Surroundings of the Temple
   Read Ezekiel 47--48.

1.   Wherever the stream of water from the Temple flows, what will it bring?

2.   What will be true of the trees on either bank of the stream?

3.   How will the twelve gates in the new Jerusalem be named?

4.   What will the city be called?

* * * * * * * * * * * * * *

324   THE ANGEL BY THE TIGRIS RIVER
   Scan Daniel 10; read 11--12.

NOTE: The setting for this vision is the third year of the reign of
         Cyrus of Persia. Also note references to Michael, Israel's
         guardian angel.

1.   What struggle did the angel describe to Daniel?

2.   What did the angel say would happen to God's people at the end
      of time?

3.   The angel said God's people had to be faithful for 1335 days.
      When does this period begin?

STORIES ABOUT DANIEL AND HIS FRIENDS
① Royal Food Refused
② Nebuchadnezzar's Dream
③ The Blazing Furnace
④ Nebuchadnezzar's Madness
⑤ Belshazzar's Banquet
⑥ Daniel in the Pit of Lions

VISIONS OF DANIEL
① The Four Beasts
② The Ram and the Goat
③ The Seventy Years
④ The Angel by the Tigris River

11. Sister prostitutes who represented Samaria and Jerusalem worshiping idols

12. Jerusalem whose faith would be purified by the fire of God's anger

13. When Jerusalem is destroyed, the survivors (too stunned for grief) will not mourn. Then they will know the Lord is God.

Check the JUST FOR FUN on the next page and follow instructions at the end of its answer page.

* * * * * * * * * * * * * *

223C

1. "Wherever it flows, it will bring life."

2. They will bear fruit every month and their leaves be used to heal people.

3. They will be named after the twelve tribes, the sons of Jacob.

NOTE: Joseph is included (not his sons) and so is Levi. The gates are named after Jacob's twelve sons.

4. The city will be called "The Lord Is Here."

Check the JUST FOR FUN on the next page and follow instructions at the end of its answer page.

* * * * * * * * * * * * * *

324

1. The kingdoms of Egypt and Syria were fighting.

NOTE: This is a remarkably circumstantial account of the wars between the Ptolemies of Egypt and the Seleucids of Syria, leading up to the attempt by the Seleucid king, Antiochus Epiphanes, to suppress the Jewish religion.

2. Those whose names are written in God's book of life will be saved and will enjoy eternal life while others will suffer eternal disgrace.

3. The period begins with the time of The Awful Horror.

NOTE: Jesus speaks of this in Matthew 24:15. Daniel first mentions it in 9:27.

Check the JUST FOR FUN on the next page and follow instructions at the end of its answer page.

Ezekiel: Signs

Find the following signs in this square. (They appear spelled forwards and backwards. They may be in horizontal, vertical, or diagonal positions.)

BRICK, HAIRCUT, REFUGEE, TREMBLING, WHITEWASH, BURNED VINE, EAGLE, SWORD, FURNACE, SISTERS, POT

Can you identify the meaning of each sign?

A	S	I	S	K	O	W	E	G	E
F	I	N	E	C	A	H	N	I	N
U	S	E	D	I	T	I	N	H	I
R	T	O	P	R	L	T	E	A	V
N	E	M	A	B	O	E	M	I	D
A	R	F	M	E	R	W	I	R	E
C	S	E	U	L	T	A	S	C	N
E	R	T	T	G	H	S	S	U	R
T	A	O	N	A	E	H	F	T	U
C	W	R	I	E	R	E	C	T	B

Check your answers on the next page.

* * * * * * * * * * * * * *

JUST FOR FUN!   Ezekiel: Mixed Terms and Priestly Lines

Try to unscramble these terms that were used or described in Ezekiel 37--48.

TRALOM NAM	YRD NEBOS	OGG FO EMCHESH DAN LABUT	DALN FO GAMGO	TRUEFU LEMTEP
GROVENIES ROLD	KAZOD NILE	FIEL VINGIG RATEMS	HANGELI VASELE	

Ezekiel 44:10-16 restricts the priesthood to priests of the line of Zadok. Other priests of the line of Levi would do subordinate work because they had not been faithful to the Lord. This was part of the priestly reform and purification of worship basic to later Judaism, for which Ezekiel prepared the way.

1. Which son of Aaron was Zadok's ancestor? (See 1 Chron. 24:3.)

2. When Zadok was faithful to David, what high priest of the other priestly line was not? (Ending the house of Eli in 1 Kings 1:7-8; 2:27)

Check answers on the next page.

* * * * * * * * * * * * * * *

JUST FOR FUN!   Daniel: Revealing Hidden Things

In the Old Testament, Daniel is the most important example of apocalyptic literature (meaning "hidden things revealed"), as Revelation is in the New Testament. The major theme of all such writing is God's revelation of the end-time, or the coming of God's kingdom.

Can you identify five words or phrases from Daniel's visions as they are hidden in these sentences?
Example: He said an "I" eloquently. (Daniel)

1. Will your choice be asters or daisies?

2. Let's go at once, or a marvelous opportunity will be lost! (Two words, but separated)

3. I'll eat the orange later.

4. I advise, "Vent your wrath on many ears." (Two words, but separated)

5. But I, grisly though I be, hear I've raised their hopes. (Two words, but separated)

Check your answers on the next page.

JUST FOR FUN Answers

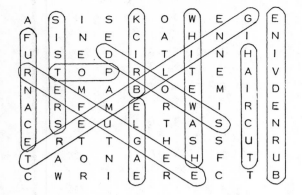

Brick (Ez. 4:1-2)--siege of Jerusalem

Haircut (Ez. 5:1)--judgment in three parts

Whitewash (Ez. 13:10)--false prophets punished

Refugee (Ez. 12:11)--Jews will be refugees

Trembling (Ez. 12:18)--Jews will be afraid

Burned vine (Ez. 15:4,6-7)--punishment of people in
                                              Jerusalem

Eagle (Ez. 17:3)--king of Babylon taking Jehoiachin

Sword (Ez. 21)--King of Babylon as God's instrument of
                                              punishment

Furnace (Ez. 22:17)--anger of the Lord

Sisters (Ez. 23)--Samaria and Jerusalem

Pot (Ez. 24:6)--Jerusalem in sin

Study the outline of Ezekiel 1--24 on page 60 and Section chart 1 for those chapters, page 85. Then take Section Test 1 on page 87.

Study the outline of Ezekiel 1--24 on page 60 and Section chart 1 for those chapters, page 85. Then take Section Test 1 on page 87.

* * * * * * * * * * * * * * *

JUST FOR FUN Answers

Mortal man	Dry bones	Gog of Meshech and Tubal	Land of Magog Future Temple
Sovereign Lord	Zadok line	Life-giving stream	Healing leaves

The line of high priests (Levi→ Aaron→ Eleazar and Ithamar→ Zadok and Abiathar→ Zadok alone) demonstrates fulfillment of the judgment promised against Eli's descendants (through Samuel when a boy in the shrine at Shiloh).

1. Eleazar

2. Abiathar

Study the outline of Ezekiel on page 60 and Section Chart 2, page 85. Then take Section Test 2 on page 88.

Study the outline of Ezekiel on page 60 and Section Chart 2, page 85. Then take Section Test 2 on page 88.

* * * * * * * * * * * * * * *

JUST FOR FUN Answers

1. <u>Be asters</u>

2. <u>go at</u> once...<u>or a marvelous</u>

3. <u>orange later</u>

4. <u>advise</u>, "<u>Vent your wrath on many ears</u>."

5. But <u>I, grisly</u> though I be, <u>hear I've raised</u>

NOTE: The King James Version translates the "one who had been living forever" in Daniel 7:9, 13, and 22 as "Ancient of days," the beginning of a well-known hymn.

Study the outline of Daniel on page 60 and Section Chart 3 on page 86. Then take Section Test 3 on page 89.

Study the outline of Daniel on page 60 and Section Chart 3 on page 86. Then take Section Test 3 on page 89.

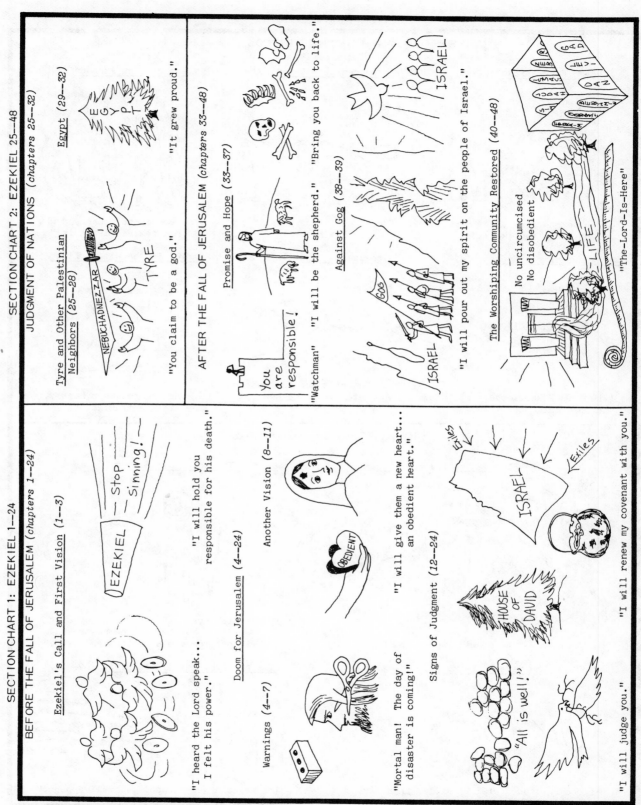

SECTION CHART 2: EZEKIEL 25—48

JUDGMENT OF NATIONS (chapters 25—32)

Egypt (29—32)

"It grew proud."

Tyre and Other Palestinian Neighbors (25—28)

NEBUCHADNEZZAR

TYRE

"You claim to be a god."

AFTER THE FALL OF JERUSALEM (chapters 33—48)

Promise and Hope (33—37)

"Bring you back to life."

"I will be the shepherd."

"Watchman"

Against Gog (38—39)

GOG

ISRAEL

ISRAEL

"I will pour out my spirit on the people of Israel."

The Worshiping Community Restored (40—48)

No uncircumcised
No disobedient

LIFE

"The-Lord-Is-Here"

SECTION CHART 1: EZEKIEL 1—24

BEFORE THE FALL OF JERUSALEM (chapters 1—24)

Ezekiel's Call and First Vision (1—3)

EZEKIEL — Stop Sinning!

"I will hold you responsible for his death."

"I heard the Lord speak...
I felt his power."

Doom for Jerusalem (4—24)

Another Vision (8—11)

OBEDIENT

"I will give them a new heart...
an obedient heart."

Warnings (4—7)

"Mortal man! The day of disaster is coming!"

Signs of Judgment (12—24)

Exiles

ISRAEL

Exiles

HOUSE OF DAVID

"All is well!"

"I will judge you."

"I will renew my covenant with you."

Study Section Chart 1. Then take Section Test 1, page 87. Study Section Chart 2 and then take Section Test 2, page 88. Study both charts before taking Unit Test 2 at the end of the study of Ezekiel and Daniel.

STORIES ABOUT DANIEL AND HIS FRIENDS *(chapters 1--6)*

Royal Food Refused *(1)*

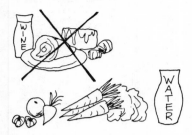

"God gave the four young men
knowledge and skill."

Nebuchadnezzar's Dream *(2)*

"Your God is the Lord
over kings."

The Blazing Furnace *(3)*

"There is no other god who
can rescue like this."

Nebuchadnezzar's Madness *(4)*

"When you acknowledge that
God rules all the world."

Belshazzar's Banquet *(5)*

"You did not honor the God
who determines whether
you live or die."

Daniel in the Pit of Lions *(6)*

"He had not been hurt ...
for he trusted God."

VISIONS OF DANIEL *(chapters 7--12)*

The Four Beasts *(7)*

"Their royal power will never end."

The Ram and the Goat *(8)*

"He will even defy the greatest King
of all, but he will be destroyed
without the use of any human power."

The Seventy Years *(9)*

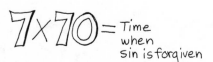

"God's chosen leader will be killed unjustly."

The Angel by the Tigris River *(10--12)*

"The great angel Michael ... will appear."

Study this chart and the outline of Daniel on page 60. Then take Section Test 3 on page 89.

SECTION TEST 1: EZEKIEL 1—24

A. STRUCTURE

Outline. Complete this outline of Ezekiel 1—24.

1. _____ the _____ of
   _____

   2. _____'s _____
       and _____ _____

   3. _____ for _____

Sequence. Number these events from 1-3 in order
as they occurred in Ezekiel.

____ Ezekiel's wife died.

____ Ezekiel was told his tongue would be paralyzed.

____ Ezekiel was called in a vision to be a
prophet.

C. PROPHECY

Signs and Visions. Write the number of the sign or
vision before the ONE term with which it is most
closely associated.

1. Brick and trenches   ____ Survivors of Jeru-
                                  salem's fall

2. Cut hair in the   ____ Samaria and Judah
   fire   both idolatrous

3. Hole-in-wall   ____ Judgment in three
   escape   stages

4. Four creatures   ____ King of Babylon
   left   ____ Siege of Jerusalem

5. Whitewashed   ____ Survivors too
   wall   stunned for grief

6. Refining furnace   ____ God's anger

7. Cedar tree   ____ Saying all is well
                        when it's not

8. Dazzling light   ____ God's restoration of
9. The Lord's sword   Israel as promised

10. Oholah and   ____ Sinful Jerusalem
    Oholibah   needing cleansing

11. Corroded pot   ____ Those disturbed by
                    Jerusalem's sin

12. Mark on forehead   ____ God's glory left the
13. Death without   Temple
    mourning   ____ God's presence

About Prophecies. Circle the ONE letter that BEST
answers each.

1. Outraged, God showed Ezekiel ALL of these forms
   of idolatry in the Temple EXCEPT:

   a. Idols at the North Gate
   b. Priests and leaders worshiping snake images
   c. Women mourning the god Tammuz
   d. The high priest giving Temple offerings to
      the god Milcom

2. God promised the exiles in Babylon that he
   would:

   a. Never punish them again
   b. Give them obedient hearts
   c. Make a new covenant
   d. b and c

3. God's glory left the Temple when Ezekiel saw:

   a. Two men murder a third
   b. Four creatures begin to fly
   c. The man shining like bronze covered by
      clouds
   d. The wheels roll to the throne

4. The king of Judah will die in Babylon because:

   a. He broke the treaty with Babylon.
   b. He offered his son in sacrifice.
   c. This sign will make people repent.
   d. a and b

5. Ezekiel did NOT say this about sour grapes:

   a. People often said this proverb.
   b. Sour grapes were people who rebelled.
   c. People thought they suffered for their
      parents' sins, not their own.
   d. Everyone would die because of his own sin.

6. Ezekiel says an evil person who stops sinning
   will:

   a. Die
   b. Be forgiven
   c. Have less punishment
   d. Teach others

7. In spite of Israel's rebellion, God will:

   a. Give the exiles a new covenant in Babylon
   b. Protect Jerusalem from attack
   c. Bring the exiles back to Israel
   d. Refrain from punishing them

D. FEATURES

Background. Complete the following statements.

1. Ezekiel lived in _____ as a prophet.
2. Ezekiel had been _____ along with
   _____.
3. Ezekiel prophesied to Jews in _____
   and _____.

Special Content. Circle the numbers of the four
items that distinguish Ezekiel from Jeremiah.

1. A plot against the prophet's life
2. "Mortal man"
3. "I heard the Lord speak....I felt his power."
4. The broken jar
5. "On the throne was a figure that looked like
   a man."
6. Most prophecies in chronological order
7. "I chose you before I gave you life."
8. "Change the way you are living."

*Check your answers, page 133. Compute your scores on page 136 and enter them on Unit 2 growth record,
page 138. Then continue with the guided reading on page 63.*

A. STRUCTURE

Outline. Complete this outline of Ezekiel 25--48.

1. _____ of _____
    2. _____ and Other _____
       _____
    3. _____
4. _____ the _____ of _____
    5. _____ and _____
    6. Against _____
    7. The _____ _____
       _____

Sequence. Number these items from 1-3 in the order in which they appear in Ezekiel 25--48.

____ The king of Tyre was called proud.

____ Ezekiel's speech was restored.

____ A survivor brought news of Jerusalem's fall.

C. PROPHECY

Signs and Visions. Write the number of the sign or vision before the ONE term with which it is most closely associated.

1. Two sticks,   ____ The new Jerusalem in the
   end to end   end-time
2. Crocodile   ____ The Lord
3. Good shepherd   ____ Judah and Israel reunited
                         in one kingdom
4. Watchman   ____ Ezekiel responsible for
5. Valley of   warning evildoers
   bones   ____ The king of Egypt
6. The Lord-Is-   ____ New life for a dead Israel
   Here

About Prophecies. Circle the letter of the ONE BEST answer for each.

1. The Lord is going to punish Tyre because:

    a. Tyre attacked Jerusalem.
    b. Tyre cheered at the fall of Jerusalem.
    c. The king of Tyre claimed to be a god.
    d. b and c

2. Egyptians will find ungodly foreigners:

    a. Throughout the land of Egypt
    b. In the world of the dead
    c. Plotting to betray Egypt
    d. Enjoying the fruits of Egyptian labor

3. The Lord holds Ezekiel responsible for:

    a. The death of any evil person he fails to warn
    b. All the sins of Israel since his call
    c. His own sin alone
    d. Making people turn from their sin

4. When Nebuchadnezzar takes Egypt, the Lord will:

    a. Punish Nebuchadnezzar
    b. Punish Israel next
    c. Make Israel strong
    d. Reunite Israel with Judah

5. Ezekiel prophesied ALL of the following EXCEPT:

    a. Gog will attack Israel from the north.
    b. Egypt will attack Magog from the south.
    c. God will send an earthquake to Israel.
    d. God will pour out his spirit on Israel at the time of the defeat of Gog.

6. When Ezekiel saw his final vision of the future, he was taken to:

    a. A high mountain in Israel
    b. The king's palace
    c. The Temple
    d. a and c

7. Ezekiel saw the man who shone like bronze:

    a. Eat a scroll
    b. Act out the desecration of the Temple
    c. Glow like fire as he approached the throne
    d. Measure the Temple

8. When Ezekiel saw the dazzling light in the new Temple, he described ALL these EXCEPT:

    a. The Lord crowned the shining man.
    b. The Lord's presence returned to the Temple.
    c. The Lord excluded all the uncircumcised and the disobedient from the Temple.
    d. The Lord excluded the Levites from the Most Holy Place.

9. Ezekiel's vision of the Temple describes ALL of the following EXCEPT:

    a. A life-giving stream flows from the Temple.
    b. Trees bear fruit each month.
    c. Gold leaves are filled with oil.
    d. People use the leaves for healing.

D. FEATURES

Background. Complete these statements.

1. Ezekiel's teaching stressed that the

    _____ is _____

    for his own sin.

2. The book of Ezekiel was written just before and

    just after the _____ of _____.

3. Like Jeremiah, Ezekiel foretold a new

    _____.

Special Content. Circle the numbers of five items that distinguish Ezekiel from most other prophets.

1. Can these bones come back to life?
2. Which is more important, the potter or the clay?
3. Wherever it flows it will bring life.
4. They will run and not get weary.
5. Mortal man
6. Is there no medicine in Gilead?
7. Because of our sins he was wounded.
8. I myself will look for my sheep and take care of them.
9. I do not enjoy seeing a sinner die.
10. Why are wicked men so prosperous?

Check your answers, page 133. Compute your scores on page 136 and enter them on the Unit 2 growth record, page 138. Then begin the study of Daniel on page 61.

SECTION TEST 3: DANIEL

A. STRUCTURE

Outline. Complete this outline of Daniel.

I. _____ About _____
and His _____
(ch.) 1. _____ _____ _____
2. _____ 's _____
3. The _____ _____
4. _____ 's _____
5. _____ 's _____
6. _____ in the _____
of _____
II. _____ of _____
(ch.) 7. The _____ _____
8. The _____ and the _____
9. The _____ _____
10. The _____ by the _____
_____

Sequence. Number these events 1–4 in the order in which they occur in Daniel.

____ A king was slain.
____ Daniel was put in charge of the king's advisers.
____ Daniel and his friends were chosen for court service.
____ A king stopped ruling for seven years.

B. NARRATIVE

Persons. Write the number of the person before the ONE term most closely associated with that person.

1. Daniel
2. Hananiah
3. Mishael
4. Azariah
5. Ashpenaz
6. Belshazzar
7. Nebuchadnezzar

____ Shadrach
____ Belteshazzar
____ Abednego
____ Meshach
____ Used Temple treasures in palace celebration
____ Insisted that the Jews eat court food
____ Ordered the death penalty for not knowing his dream

Events. Circle the ONE BEST answer for each.

1. When given the death penalty, Daniel did NOT:
   a. Obtain royal permission for more time
   b. Ask God to reveal the dream
   c. Fast two days while praying
   d. Tell Nebuchadnezzar what God revealed

2. At the king's feast, a human hand wrote:
   a. Daniel and his friends had to be freed.
   b. Belshazzar's rule was ending.
   c. All people must know that the Lord is God.
   d. Belshazzar's son would die.

3. When Daniel's friends refused to worship the statue, ALL of these happened EXCEPT:
   a. The king had them beaten.
   b. They were thrown into a blazing furnace.
   c. One who looked like a god was seen with them.
   d. The king promoted them.

4. Nebuchadnezzar regained his mind and rule when:
   a. He asked Daniel to advise him.
   b. He agreed to make Daniel's God the official God of Babylon.
   c. He freed his son from prison.
   d. He admitted that God rules the world.

5. When Daniel kept on praying, ALL of these happened EXCEPT:
   a. Darius tried to protect Daniel.
   b. Daniel was thrown into the lions' pit.
   c. The king ordered Babylon to fear God.
   d. Daniel took the king's place and ruled.

C. PROPHECY

Check your answers to the outline under "A. STRUCTURE." Then write the number of the vision or sign as listed in that outline (the chapter number) before the ONE sentence or phrase most closely associated with it. (Turn the page for Visions.)

Signs.

____ God revealed the dream and its meaning.
____ A hand wrote foretelling the end of a reign.
____ Daniel broke Darius's rule by praying.
____ An experiment proved the Jews to be stronger.
____ A tall tree was chopped down in the dream.
____ Shadrach, Meshach, and Abednego were punished.

Visions.

_____ God will give his people unending royal power.

_____ Those named in God's book will live forever.

_____ It means weeks of years, 490 years until the final restoration of Jerusalem.

_____ The destructive king would be destroyed without use of human power.

D. FEATURES

Background. Complete the following statements.

1. Daniel is listed among the _____ in the Jewish canon.

2. Traditionally Daniel is dated as written in the time of the _____.

3. Most modern scholars date the writing of Daniel in the time of the _____.

4. Daniel is known for its _____ writing.

5. In Daniel Israel's view of God changes from the God of _____

6. to the Lord of _____.

Special Content. Circle the numbers of six items from Daniel that distinguish Daniel from Ezekiel.

1. There is no other god who can rescue like this.
2. You did not honor the God who determines whether you live or die.
3. I heard the Lord speak....I felt his power.
4. On the throne ... a figure that looked like a man ...
5. Wherever it flows it will bring life.
6. Angels Gabriel and Michael
7. Can these bones come back to life?
8. Their royal power will never end.
9. I do not enjoy seeing a sinner die.
10. God's chosen leader will be killed unjustly.
11. He had not been hurt at all for he trusted God.
12. The Lord-Is-Here

Check your answers on page 133. Compute your scores on page 137 and record them on the Unit 2 growth record on page 138. Study any items you have missed. Then review the section charts and outlines of Ezekiel and Daniel before taking Unit Test 2.

UNIT TEST 2: EZEKIEL AND DANIEL

A. STRUCTURE

Outline. Complete the following outlines.

EZEKIEL

1. _____ the _____ of _____
2. _____ of _____
3. _____ the _____ of _____

DANIEL

4. _____ About _____ and His _____
5. _____ of _____

Sequence. Number these events from 1-6 for Ezekiel and 1-5 for Daniel to show the order in which they appear in these books.

_____ Ezekiel was told he would lose his speech.

_____ Ezekiel regained his power of speech.

_____ Ezekiel was called to be a prophet.

_____ Ezekiel's wife died.

_____ A survivor brought news of Jerusalem's fall.

_____ Ezekiel was brought to Babylon as a captive.

_____ Daniel was made third in power.

_____ A king stopped ruling for seven years.

_____ Daniel was put over the king's advisers.

_____ Daniel and his friends were chosen for court service.

_____ Three friends risked death to obey God.

B. NARRATIVE

Persons. Write the number of the person before the ONE term that best identifies the person.

1. Ezekiel   _____ Ruler from Magog
2. Daniel   _____ Abednego
3. Hananiah   _____ Priest
4. Mishael   _____ Meshach
5. Azariah   _____ Belteshazzar
6. Ashpenaz   _____ King
7. Belshazzar   _____ Shadrach
8. Gog   _____ Babylonian official

Events. Circle the letter of the ONE BEST answer.

1. Ezekiel did NOT:

   a. Lose his wife in Babylon
   b. Join the Babylonian king's staff
   c. Prophesy to the Jerusalem Jews
   d. Prophesy to the exiles in Babylon

2. Daniel and his friends were ordered killed:

   a. Because the magicians didn't know the dream
   b. So Daniel asked his friends to pray
   c. So Daniel and his friends fasted two days
   d. a and b

(continued on page 91)

3. Shadrach, Meshach, and Abednego were put in the furnace because:

    a. They refused to bow down to a statue.
    b. Their enemies had substituted them for condemned prisoners.
    c. They refused to honor God.
    d. They refused to worship the king.

4. The dream of the tall tree did NOT mean that:

    a. Nebuchadnezzar was a very great king.
    b. The king would lose his mind.
    c. The king would be exiled the rest of his life.
    d. The king would admit God controlled kingdoms.

5. Numbers, weight, and divisions were part of:

    a. The news that Belshazzar's rule was over.
    b. Daniel's vision of the last days.
    c. The writing on the wall
    d. a and c

6. After Daniel's jealous enemies obtained an order from the king against prayer:

    a. Darius regretted it.
    b. Darius punished Daniel.
    c. The lions did not hurt Daniel.
    d. a, b, and c

C. PROPHECY

Signs. Write the number of the sign before the ONE term most closely associated with it.

1. Brick and trenches
2. Cut hair put in fire
3. Escape by hole in wall
4. Whitewashed wall
5. Refining furnace
6. Cedar
7. The Lord's sword
8. Oholah and Oholibah
9. Corroded pot
10. Death of Ezekiel's wife

____ Survivors of Jerusalem's fall
____ Sinful Jerusalem
____ Idolatrous Samaria and Judah
____ Judgment in three stages
____ King of Babylon
____ Siege of Jerusalem
____ Great suffering when Jerusalem falls
____ God's anger
____ Saying all is well when it's not
____ God's restoration of Israel

Signs (continued).

11. Nebuchadnezzar's dream
12. Two sticks, end to end
13. Refusal of royal food
14. Crocodile
15. Blazing furnace
16. Nebuchadnezzar's madness
17. Good shepherd
18. Belshazzar's banquet
19. Watchman
20. The pit of lions

____ The Lord
____ Judah and Israel reunited in one kingdom
____ Ezekiel's responsibility for warning evildoers
____ King of Egypt
____ God revealed the content and its meaning.
____ Writing on the wall about the end of the reign
____ Daniel prayed, breaking Darius's law.
____ Experiment proved the Jews to be stronger.
____ A tall tree chopped down with its stump chained
____ Shadrach, Meshach, and Abednego refused to worship the statue.

Visions. Write the number of the vision before the ONE term most closely associated with it.

1. Seventy years
2. Four creatures flying
3. Ram and goat
4. Valley of bones
5. Dazzling light
6. Mark on forehead
7. Stream flowing from the Temple
8. Angel by the Tigris
9. The Lord-Is-Here
10. Four beasts

____ God's presence
____ Jerusalem in the end-time
____ Those disturbed by Jerusalem's sin
____ God's glory leaving Jerusalem
____ Bringing life wherever it goes
____ God's people receiving unending royal power
____ Those named in God's book to be saved
____ New life for a dead Israel
____ In 490 years: Jerusalem's final restoration
____ King destroyed without human power

About Prophecies. Circle the letter of the ONE BEST answer for each.

1. God was particularly outraged at the idolatry:

    a. Because the priests did not stop the people
    b. Because it was practiced in his Temple
    c. Because offerings were given to Milcom
    d. Because children were sacrificed

2. When the light moved above the four creatures:

    a. God's glory left the Temple.
    b. The man shone brighter.
    c. The wheels rolled to the throne.
    d. A dark cloud hovered over Ezekiel.

(continued on page 92)

3. Concerning the king of Judah's treaty with Nebuchadnezzar, ALL of the following are true EXCEPT:

   a. The treaty kept Judah quiet and docile.
   b. The king of Judah sent to Egypt for an army.
   c. The king of Judah broke the treaty.
   d. Nebuchadnezzar caught the king in a net.

4. God promised the exiles in Babylon that he would:

   a. Bring them back to Israel
   b. Rebuild the Temple
   c. Protect Jerusalem from attack
   d. b and c

5. The Lord would make Israel strong when:

   a. The priests purified the Temple
   b. Syria attacked Jerusalem
   c. Nebuchadnezzar conquered Egypt
   d. All people kept the law

6. Ezekiel claims that Gog will:

   a. Invade Israel
   b. Form an alliance with Egypt
   c. Rule Judah and her neighbors for many years
   d. a and c

7. The Lord's presence returned to the Temple when:

   a. The shining man entered the Most Holy Place.
   b. The figure on the throne spoke.
   c. The dazzling light appeared.
   d. All people confessed their sins.

8. The trees on either side of the stream:

   a. Bear fruit for food every month
   b. Shade God's people from all sin
   c. Have leaves that do not wither
   d. a and c

Write the number of the prophecy before the ONE term most closely associated with it.

9. Final vision of the future

10. In the world of the dead

11. Tyre's punishment

12. Measuring the Temple

13. New covenant

14. Receive life

15. Individual is responsible for own sin

_____ Gives God's people new hearts

_____ Sour grapes proverb forbidden

_____ Evil who stop sinning

_____ Taken to the Temple

_____ Celebrating the fall of Jerusalem

_____ Ungodly people of other nations

_____ Man who shone like bronze

D. FEATURES

Write E for Ezekiel or D for Daniel before EACH special item.

Background.

_____ Exiled along with Jehoiachin

_____ Strongly influenced later Judaism

_____ Listed among the Writings in the Jewish canon

_____ Known for its apocalyptic writing

_____ Prophesied to exiles in Babylon

_____ Saw God as Lord of world history

_____ Mostly doom for Jerusalem and judgment for the nations

_____ Most modern scholars date the writing in the Maccabean period.

_____ Prophesied to the people of Jerusalem

_____ Foretold a new covenant

_____ Stressed the individual's responsibility for his own sin

_____ About half the book is written in Aramaic.

_____ Part was written before the fall of Jerusalem.

Special Content. Write E or D before EACH item. One item is both E and D.

_____ I heard the Lord speak....I felt his power.

_____ Mortal man (son of man)

_____ No other god who can rescue like this

_____ On the throne ... a figure that looked like a man

_____ The watchman

_____ You did not honor the God who determines whether you live or die.

_____ He had not been hurt at all, for he trusted God.

_____ Angels Gabriel and Michael

_____ Can these bones come back to life?

_____ Wherever it flows it will bring life.

_____ Their royal power will never end.

_____ God's chosen leader will be killed unjustly.

Check your answers on pages 133–134. Compute your scores on page 137 and enter them on the Unit 2 growth record on page 138. Look up any answers you missed, using the references given on the answer page. Then read the objectives for Unit 3 on page 93.

UNIT 3: THE TWELVE

OBJECTIVES

In Unit 3, as in Units 1 and 2, items you are to learn have been classified in four categories: structure, narrative, prophecy, and features. These are defined on page 5.

Upon completion of Unit 3 you will be able to do at least 90% of the following:

1. State the major headings of each of the twelve books of the minor prophets.
2. Associate at least 6 persons and 4 places mentioned in these books with roles or events.
3. Associate 12 signs or visions described in these books with their meanings.
4. Identify 21 statements about prophecies from these books.
5. State 15 background facts about these books.
6. Identify the source of 4 special content items and 16 well-known or significant quotations.

INSTRUCTIONS

Each page of guided reading in Unit 3 is divided by asterisks into four "frames." DO NOT READ ALL THE WAY DOWN THE PAGE, but turn the page after reading a single frame. Proceed as follows:

1. Take the Unit 3 pre-test and record your score. On this and all tests wording may usually vary if the meaning is the same.
2. Study the introduction and outline as you begin each book.
3. Note the number and heading of each frame.
4. Read the questions in each frame first.
5. Read the Bible passages assigned. When asked to scan a passage, you may skip it, skim over it, or read it.
6. Try to answer the questions from memory. Just say the answers to yourself. You may write them if you wish, but it will double the time required.
7. When in doubt, look at the Bible to finish answering questions.
8. Then and ONLY THEN turn the page to check your answers. Exact wording does not usually matter.

9. Note the drawings to help remember major points.
10. Do the Just for Funs if you enjoy them and have time. Be sure to follow the instructions at the end of the frame even if you skip them.
11. Use section charts plus outlines to review the structure and major themes of each book.
12. Take section tests as instructed, check answers, and record your scores in the back of this book. Then return to page 97 to begin guided reading for the next biblical book.
13. Take the unit test, check answers, and record your scores on the growth record.
14. As you check unit test answers, look up the references for any questions you miss.
15. Complete the Unit 2 growth record on page 138 and figure your growth in knowledge of the content of the twelve minor prophets.

Now begin the pre-test for Unit 3 on page 94.

A. STRUCTURE

Write the number of the book of prophecy before the major divisions of that book.

1. Hosea
2. Joel
3. Amos
4. Obadiah
5. Jonah
6. Micah
7. Nahum
8. Habakkuk
9. Zephaniah
10. Haggai
11. Zechariah
12. Malachi

_____ Punishment of Edom; Day of the Lord

_____ Judgment of Ninevah; Fall of Ninevah

_____ Israel's sins; God's judgment and mercy

_____ Rebuild the Temple; Promise to Zerubbabel

_____ Disobeys; Prays; Obeys; Is angry and God merciful

_____ Prophet's marriage; Israel's crimes; Repentance and promise

_____ Day of the Lord; Doom of neighbors; Doom of Jerusalem and redemption

_____ Locusts; Restoration; Day of the Lord

_____ Prophecies; Messiah and future deliverance

_____ Messages to all nations; Messages to Israel

_____ Dialogue with God; Doom on unrighteous; Prayer for mercy

_____ Judgment on neighbors; Israel's judgment; Five visions

B. NARRATIVE

Persons. Write the number of the person before the ONE term most closely associated with that person.

1. Amaziah
2. Jeroboam II
3. Gomer
4. Joel
5. Jonah
6. Nahum
7. Zerubbabel
8. Joshua
9. Obadiah

_____ Freedom from Israel's enemy

_____ Preached judgment on mountainous nation

_____ Unfaithful wife

_____ King given bad report of Amos

_____ High Priest

_____ Ran away from God

_____ Crops destroyed all through the land

_____ Wanted Amos to go back to Judah

_____ Governor of Judah after the return

Places. Write the number of the place before the ONE term most closely associated with it.

1. Edom
2. Bethel
3. Tekoa
4. Ninevah
5. Judah
6. Israel

_____ Home of Amaziah

_____ Nation that succumbed to Assyria

_____ Even the animals fasted

_____ Amos's hometown

_____ To be punished, then ruled by Jerusalem

_____ Country that Amos left to prophesy to another

C. PROPHECY

Signs and Visions. Write the number of the sign or vision before its meaning. Two of the visions (the second group) have the same meaning.

1. Silly pigeon
2. Half-baked loaf
3. Plague of locusts
4. Hosea's marriage
5. Child named "Unloved"
6. Two shepherds
7. Riding on a donkey
8. Gomer
9. Child named "Jezreel"
10. Fast-growing plant that died

_____ Future king of peace

_____ Day of the Lord

_____ End of Jehu's line

_____ Idolatrous Israel

_____ Israel calls on Egypt and then Assyria for help

_____ God's relationship with Israel

_____ God and a wicked one as leaders of God's people

_____ God's compassion

_____ God could no longer love Israel.

_____ Relying on others took Israel's strength away.

Signs and Visions (continued).

11. Locusts, fire
12. Baskets of fruit
13. Horses
14. Horns and workers
15. Lampstand, olive trees
16. Measuring line
17. Stone with seven facets
18. Plumb line

_____ Overthrow of nations that opposed Judah

_____ Jerusalem restored

_____ Eyes of the Lord and his anointed leaders

_____ The end of Israel

_____ God's people out of line, will be punished

_____ God will remove Israel's sin in one day.

_____ Destruction of Israel (averted by prayer)

About Prophecies. Circle the letter of the ONE BEST answer for each prophecy.

1. Hosea. God will be the source of all Israel's blessings when:
   a. Israel worships God alone.
   b. Israel returns from exile.
   c. He makes Israel into a mighty nation.
   d. He punishes their enemies.

2. Joel. The Lord tells _____ to prepare for war.
   a. Israel
   b. Judah
   c. Egypt
   d. The nations

3. Amos. God did not send fires to destroy Israel because:
   a. He decided to send locusts.
   b. Amos prayed for Israel.
   c. The people changed their ways.
   d. The people repented in sackcloth.

4. Obadiah. Edom would be punished for:
   a. Taking advantage of Jerusalem's disaster
   b. Attacking Jerusalem
   c. Betraying escapees from Jerusalem
   d. a and c

5. <u>Jonah</u>. When Jonah preached:
   a. The people fasted.
   b. The animals fasted.
   c. The people wore sackcloth.
   d. a, b, and c

6. <u>Micah</u>. Priests, prophets, and government
   leaders:
   a. Were betraying their country
   b. Were taking bribes
   c. Were renewing their covenant with God
   d. a and b

7. <u>Nahum</u>. The leader from Ninevah:
   a. Forced his god on Israel
   b. Made plans against Israel's God
   c. Waited for Israel to turn against God
   d. Was exiled and killed

8. <u>Habakkuk</u>. How wonderful to hear:
   a. The great things God has done for his people
   b. That Nineveh has fallen
   c. The Word of the Lord
   d. a and c

9. <u>Zephaniah</u>. The people of Jerusalem would no
   longer need to be afraid because:
   a. God's power gives them victory.
   b. God will give them a strong army.
   c. God will remove their enemies.
   d. a and c

10. <u>Haggai</u>. The people are building their own
    houses:
    a. So they have left the Temple in ruins
    b. So they are not prosperous
    c. After they have rebuilt the Temple
    d. a and b

11. <u>Zechariah</u>. God promised Zerubbabel that:
    a. God's spirit would help him finish the
       Temple.
    b. God's spirit would anoint him to rule
       forever.
    c. He would be saved from the destruction.
    d. He would lead his people to victory.

12. <u>Malachi</u>. The people cheat God by:
    a. Staying away from Temple worship
    b. Using false weights
    c. Not paying their tithes
    d. Lying to the priests

D. FEATURES

<u>Background</u>. Complete the following statements.

1. Hosea's _____ was a _____ _____
   of God's love.

2. _____ _____ is the
   major theme in Amos.

3. The book of Jonah condemns _____

4. and extols God's _____ for all.

5. Joel probably lived in the _____ period.

6. Micah blamed the _____ for Judah's judgment.

7. Haggai and Zechariah urged _____ of
   the _____.

8. Zechariah prophesied the _____ _____.

9. Malachi wrote to inspire _____ _____.

Before EACH of the ten prophets below write the
number of the century B.C. in which he prophesied.
(The dates will be approximate. Scholars do not
agree on dates for Joel or Jonah. Either of two
centuries may be correct for Obadiah.)

_____ Hosea
_____ Obadiah   _____ Micah
_____ Nahum   _____ Habakkuk
_____ Zephaniah   _____ Haggai
_____ Amos   _____ Zechariah
                       _____ Malachi

<u>Special Content</u>. Write the name of the prophet
before the ONE distinguishing item.

1. _____ A large fish
2. _____ Let justice flow like a stream....
3. _____ Your king is coming ... riding on
   a donkey.
4. _____ Half-baked loaf and silly flitting pigeon.
5. _____ They paid me thirty pieces of
   silver as my wages.
6. _____ How can I give you up, Israel?
7. _____ A poem of celebration
8. _____ What he requires of us ... do what
   is just ... show ... love ...
9. _____ The Lord is in his holy Temple.
10. _____ Do what is right and humble your-
    selves before the Lord.
11. _____ I ... called him out of Egypt as
    my son.
12. _____ Before that day of the Lord ...
    I will send Elijah.
13. _____ I will pour out my spirit on
    everyone.
14. _____ Evil men get the better of the
    righteous.
15. _____ I will send my messenger to
    prepare the way for me.
16. _____ A plumb line and a basket of fruit
17. _____ My saving power will rise on you
    like the sun and bring healing
    like the sun's rays.
18. _____ The army of locusts as a sign of
    the Day of the Lord
19. _____ The new Temple more splendid than
    the old
20. _____ Hammer the points of your plows
    into swords.
21. _____ They will hammer their swords into
    plows.
22. _____ Your old men will have dreams and
    your young men will see visions.
23. _____ The people ... have sinned ... for
    this I will punish them.
24. _____ My people have broken the covenant
    ... their enemies will pursue them.

*Check your answers on page 134. Compute your
scores on page 137, and enter them on the Unit 3
growth record on page 138. You are then ready to
begin the study of Unit 3.*

OUTLINES

HOSEA

111	HOSEA'S MARRIAGE, A LIVING PARABLE	*(1--3)*
112	ISRAEL'S CRIMES AND PUNISHMENT	*(4--13)*
113	REPENTANCE AND PROMISE	*(14)*

JOEL

121	THE PLAGUE OF LOCUSTS	*(1:1--2:17)*
122	PROMISE OF RESTORATION	*(2:18-27)*
123	THE DAY OF THE LORD	*(2:28--3:21)*

AMOS

211	JUDGMENT: ISRAEL'S NEIGHBORS AND ISRAEL	*(1--2)*
212	WARNINGS TO ISRAEL	*(3--6)*
213	FIVE VISIONS	*(7--9)*
	213A Locusts, Fire and Plumb Line	
	213B Historical Note: Amos and Amaziah	
	213C Basket of Fruit and Altar	
	213D Postscript: Future Restoration	

OBADIAH

221	THE PUNISHMENT OF EDOM	*(vss. 1-14)*
222	THE DAY OF THE LORD	*(vss. 15-21)*

JONAH

231	JONAH DISOBEYS THE LORD	*(1)*
232	JONAH'S PRAYER	*(2)*
233	JONAH OBEYS THE LORD	*(3)*
234	JONAH'S ANGER AND GOD'S MERCY	*(4)*

MICAH

311	MESSAGES TO ALL NATIONS	*(1--5)*
	311A Judgment of Israel and Judah	
	311B Restoration and Universal Peace	
312	MESSAGES TO ISRAEL: WARNING AND HOPE	*(6--9)*

NAHUM

321	JUDGMENT ON NINEVEH	*(1)*
322	THE FALL OF NINEVEH	*(2--3)*

HABAKKUK

331	HABAKKUK'S DIALOGUE WITH GOD	*(1:1--2:4)*
332	DOOM ON THE UNRIGHTEOUS	*(2:5-20)*
333	HABAKKUK'S PRAYER	*(3)*

ZEPHANIAH

341	THE DAY OF THE LORD	*(1:1--2:3)*
342	DOOM OF ISRAEL'S NEIGHBORS	*(2:4-15)*
343	JERUSALEM'S DOOM AND REDEMPTION	*(3)*

HAGGAI

411	REBUILD THE TEMPLE!	*(1:1--2:19)*
412	THE PROMISE TO ZERUBBABEL	*(2:20-23)*

ZECHARIAH

421	PROPHECIES FROM THE TIME OF ZERUBBABEL	*(1--8)*
422	THE MESSIAH AND FUTURE DELIVERANCE	*(9--14)*

MALACHI

431	ISRAEL'S SINS	*(1:1--2:16)*
432	GOD'S JUDGMENT AND MERCY	*(2:17--4:6)*

NOTE: You are asked to memorize all headings except those with a letter after the numeral. To help you learn the outlines, structure drawings of scrolls will be used for each book. Each time a new heading is introduced, it is added to the scroll, beginning at the top and moving down.

110 INTRODUCTION TO HOSEA

Hosea (sounds like "hoe, SAY uh") was a prophet in the Northern Kingdom (Israel) just before the fall of Samaria to Assyria in 721 B.C. Hosea's words recall God's choice of Israel as his people in the deliverance from Egypt. He was the first prophet to use marriage as a symbol of God's relationship with his people. Israel was like the faithless wife Gomer. In this parable, Hosea's marriage was a sign of God's great love for his people.

Hosea lived in the late eighth century as a contemporary of Isaiah in Judah and also of Amos. Like Amos, he prophesied judgment for Israel, but Hosea's concern focused on Israel's apostasy.

Study the outline of Hosea opposite. Then turn to 110 on the next page.

* * * * * * * * * * * * * *

210 INTRODUCTION TO AMOS

Amos was a prophet from Tekoa (like "the BO-a") in Judah. About 750 B.C. when Jeroboam II ruled the prosperous Northern Kingdom, God sent Amos to warn Israel of the coming judgment. Many in Israel were rich because they oppressed the poor. When they worshiped God they used meaningless words and had no intention of obeying the Lord. Amos preached judgment on the Day of the Lord and urged the people of Israel to repent and treat their fellow Israelites with justice. This was their only hope for God's mercy. Amos is known for his preaching of social justice, the responsibility that special privilege brings.

Study the outline of Amos opposite. Then turn to 210 on the next page.

* * * * * * * * * * * * * *

310 INTRODUCTION TO MICAH

Micah of Judah was a contemporary of Isaiah and of Hosea in the late eighth century. We know very little about Micah. He prophesied the same ruin for Judah that Amos saw coming to Israel. Micah saw the nation's leaders as major culprits and reprimanded them soundly. Other oracles in the book of Micah, which many scholars believe are later developments of the Micah tradition, announce the Lord's salvation and compassion for his people. These passages speak of those who will be left (the remnant) and foretell the birth of the King of Peace in Bethlehem.

Study the outline of Micah opposite. Then turn to 310 on the next page.

* * * * * * * * * * * * * *

410 INTRODUCTION TO HAGGAI

Haggai (like "HAG eye"), the first of the prophets of the restoration, dated his work in 520 B.C., just five years before the Second Temple was completed. This book is addressed primarily to the governor of Judah and to its high priest. It emphasizes rebuilding the Temple. Zerubbabel (like Zeh RUB a bell) was governor of Judah under the Persian emperor Darius, and Joshua was the High Priest. Many thought that Zerubbabel would be the promised Messiah. Messianic hope appears in Haggai in the focus on the Temple and in the promise to Zerubbabel.

Study the outline of Haggai opposite. Then turn to 410 on the next page.

110   INTRODUCTION TO HOSEA

Complete these statements and then check your answers upside down at the end of the frame.

1. Hosea prophesied in _____in the _____century B.C.

2. Hosea's prophecies are concerned with Israel's _____.

3. His _____was a parable of God's love for _____.

4. Hosea was written when _____was threatening Israel just before the fall of _____in 721 B.C.

Answers: 1. Israel, eighth; 2. apostasy; 3. marriage, Israel; 4. Assyria, Samaria

Continue with 111 on the next page.

* * * * * * * * * * * * * *

210   INTRODUCTION TO AMOS

Complete these statements and then check your answers upside down below.

1. Amos came from _____in _____.

2. He lived in the middle of the _____century B.C.

3. Amos preached _____to_____.

4. He stressed the need for social_____, the _____that privilege entails.

Answers: 1. Tekoa, Judah; 2. eighth; 3. Judgement, Israel (N.K.); 4. justice, responsibility

Continue with 211 on the next page.

* * * * * * * * * * * * * *

310   INTRODUCTION TO MICAH

Complete these statements and then check the answers upside down below.

1. Micah lived in _____in the _____century B.C.

2. Micah preached _____on Judah, especially on its _____.

3. Great confidence is expressed in the Lord's _____.

Answers: 1. Judah, eighth; 2. judgement, leaders; 3. salvation or compassion

Continue with 311A on the next page.

* * * * * * * * * * * * * *

410   INTRODUCTION TO HAGGAI

Complete these statements. Then check answers upside down below.

1. This work was written in the _____century B.C.

2. Haggai emphasizes the _____of Jerusalem, especially the _____.

3. Zerubbabel was the _____of Judah and _____the High Priest.

4. Many Jews thought that Zerubbabel would be the _____.

Answers: 1. sixth; 2. restoration (or rebuilding), Temple; 3. governor, Joshua; 4. Messiah

Continue with 411 on the next page.

111   HOSEA'S MARRIAGE, A LIVING PARABLE (chapters 1--3)

     Read Hosea 1--3.

1. Why was each of Hosea's children so named?

2. For what will the Lord punish Israel?

3. The Lord said Israel was a prostitute like Gomer. Hosea was told to treat Gomer as the Lord did Israel. What does the Lord want Hosea to do to his wife who is committing adultery?

NOTE: These chapters stress the relation between Hosea's life and his prophecy.

Turn to 111 on the next page.

* * * * * * * * * * * * * *

211   JUDGMENT: ISRAEL'S NEIGHBORS AND ISRAEL (chapters 1--2)

     Read Amos 1--2.

1. Each of the eight oracles against eight nations begins with the same indictment. What is it?

2. The oracles to seven of the nations end with the same punishment. What is it?

3. After accusing Israel of social injustice, the Lord reminds them of what he has done for them. What does he accuse them of doing to the Nazirites and the prophets?

* * * * * * * * * * * * * *

311   MESSAGES TO ALL NATIONS (chapters 1--5)

311A   Judgment of Israel and Judah

     Read Micah 1--3.

1. Who is to blame for Israel's rebellion? Judah's idolatry?

2. The prophet speaks out against those who oppress the poor. After Israel and Judah have been taken away captives, what will God do for the people?

3. Why are three groups of leaders accused by Micah?

* * * * * * * * * * * * * *

411   REBUILD THE TEMPLE! (chapters 1:1--2:19)

     Read Haggai 1:1--2:19.

1. Why does the Lord say that the people are not successful in building their new lives in Judah?

2. After inspiring everyone to rebuild the Temple, what reassurance does the Lord give them about the building?

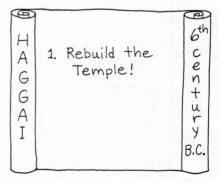

1. "Jezreel" because the Lord would soon put an end to Jehu's dynasty because of the murders that Jehu committed at Jezreel.
   "Unloved" because the Lord would no longer show love to the people of Israel nor forgive them; however, he would show love to Judah.
   "Not-My-People" because the people of Israel are not the Lord's people.

2. "For the times that she forgot me, when she burned incense to Baal and put on her jewelry to go chasing after her lovers."

3. Love her as the Lord loves Israel

* * * * * * * * * * * * * *

211

1. "The people of _____ have sinned again and again, and for this I will certainly punish them."

2. "So I will send fire upon _____ and burn down the fortresses of _____ ."

3. They made the Nazirites drink wine and ordered the prophets not to speak the Lord's message.

* * * * * * * * * * * * * *

311A

1. Samaria and Jerusalem, the capitals

2. Lead them out of exile to go free

3. The cities' rulers, priests, and prophets all work for bribes.

* * * * * * * * * * * * * *

411

1. They have worked only for themselves, leaving God's Temple in ruins.

2. It will be more splendid than the old Temple.

Unsuccessful lives

112   ISRAEL'S CRIMES AND PUNISHMENT (chapters 4--13)

Read Hosea 4:1--10; scan 4:11--5:15; read 6--7.

1. The Lord's complaint is against the priests who reject his teaching and worship idols. How do both people and priests fail in their regard for the Lord God?

2. The Lord will abandon his people until they suffer enough to look for him. What does the Lord want from his people instead of animal sacrifices and burnt offerings?

3. What does the prophet mean when he says the Lord describes Israel as a half-baked loaf of bread?

4. Why is Israel described as flitting around like a silly pigeon?

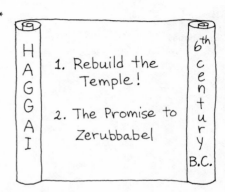

HOSEA

1. Hosea's Marriage: A Living Parable

2. Israel's Crimes and Punishment

8th century B.C.

* * * * * * * * * * * * * *

212   WARNINGS TO ISRAEL (chapters 3--6)

Read Amos 3; scan 4; read 5; scan 6.

1. Why are Israel's sins so terrible?

2. When God punishes Israel, what altars will he destroy?

3. Amos condemns the easy life of the well-to-do because they enjoy life without responsibility or compassion. Concerning the crimes of these people against those less fortunate, what does the Lord tell them to hate and to love?

4. The Lord says, "I hate your religious festivals;...I will not accept...animals..." What does God want instead?

AMOS

1. Judgment: Israel's Neighbors and Israel

2. Warnings to Israel

8th century B.C.

* * * * * * * * * * * * * *

311B   Restoration and Universal Peace

Read Micah 4--5.

NOTE: Micah contains the reverse of Joel 3:10: Plows are hammered to swords in Joel, but swords into plows in Micah, as he describes universal peace.

1. In the first passage describing the Lord ruling from Mt. Zion, what has the Lord Almighty promised?

2. The future ruler of Israel, who would bring peace, would come from an ancient family line. In what town would he be born?

* * * * * * * * * * * * * *

412   THE PROMISE TO ZERUBBABEL (chapter 2:20-23)

Read Haggai 2:20-23.

The Lord was planning to overthrow kings and end their powers. Who will the Lord appoint to rule in his name on that day?

HAGGAI

1. Rebuild the Temple!

2. The Promise to Zerubbabel

6th century B.C.

112

1. "The people do not acknowledge me as God."

2. "I want your constant love....I would rather have my people know me."

3. "They rely on the nations around them and do not realize that this...has robbed them of their strength."

4. First Israel calls on Egypt for help and then on Assyria.

* * * * * * * * * * * * * *

212

1. Israel is the only nation that the Lord knew and cared for.

2. The altars at Bethel

3. "Hate what is evil, love what is right ..."

    ("and see that justice prevails in the courts.")

4. "Let justice flow like a stream, and righteousness like a river that never goes dry."

* * * * * * * * * * * * * *

311B

1. He promised that everyone will live in peace among his own vineyards.

2. Bethlehem of Judah

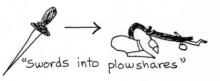

* * * * * * * * * * * * * *

412

Zerubbabel

112   ISRAEL'S CRIMES AND PUNISHMENT *(continued)*

    Scan Hosea 8:1--10:8; read 10:9--11:12; scan 12--13.

5. When God harnessed Israel for harder work, what did Israel plant instead of righteousness and reap instead of blessings?

6. When Israel was a child, what did the Lord do?

NOTE: Matthew refers to this verse as being fulfilled when Jesus fled to Egypt to live until Herod died.

7. As the people of Israel insist on turning away from God, what does the Lord find impossible to do? Why?

PROPHET OF ISRAEL
(Northern Kingdom)
8th century B.C.

* * * * * * * * * * * * *

213   FIVE VISIONS

213A Locusts, Fire and Plumb Line

    Read Amos 7:1-9.

1. Why did the Lord change his mind about destroying the land by locusts and fire?

2. The plumb line showed that the Lord would punish Israel. What dynasty would come to an end?

AMOS
1. Judgment: Israel's Neighbors and Israel
2. Warnings to Israel
3. Five Visions
8th century B.C.

* * * * * * * * * * * * *

312   MESSAGES TO ISRAEL: WARNING AND HOPE

    Read Micah 6--7.

NOTE the courtroom image used in the "Lord's case against Israel."

1. Instead of calves or olive oil to pay for our sins, what does the Lord require of us?

2. How were the evil men exploiting the poor?

3. Micah was confident that the Lord would save his people. In what ways did he see the Lord as different from other gods?

MICAH
1. Messages to All Nations
2. Messages to Israel: Warning and Hope
8th century B.C.

* * * * * * * * * * * * *

420   INTRODUCTION TO ZECHARIAH

Zechariah prophesied at the same time as Haggai. (Both prophets are mentioned in Ezra 5 and 6.) Rather than using exhortations, as did Haggai, Zechariah described visions and their interpretations. The Branch and the two anointed men are visions which combine Zechariah's strong messianic hope with priestly interpretations. The first eight chapters are dated from 520 - 518 B.C., but the collection of messages about the expected Messiah and the final judgment are not dated. Most contemporary scholars think that these last six chapters were written during the Greek period. Others think they are pre-exilic, and some maintain that Zechariah wrote the entire book or still defend the unity of the entire book.

5. Israel planted evil and reaped its harvest, war and death.

6. God loved Israel and "called him out of Egypt as my son."

7. "How can I give you up, Israel?...My love for you is too strong."

NOTE: Chapter 11 has a strong parent-son image.

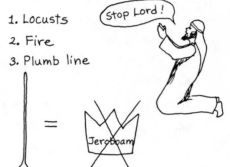

* * * * * * * * * * * * * *

213A

1. Amos prayed for Israel.

2. King Jeroboam's dynasty

1. Locusts
2. Fire
3. Plumb line

Stop Lord!

Jeroboam

* * * * * * * * * * * * * *

312

1. "To do what is just, to show constant love, and to live in
    humble fellowship with our God."

2. Using false scales and weights

3. "You forgive the sins of your people who have survived....You
    take pleasure in showing us your constant love. You will
    be merciful to us once again."

The Lord's case against Israel

FALSE

* * * * * * * * * * * * * *

420   INTRODUCTION TO ZECHARIAH

Complete the following statements; then check answers upside down at the end of the frame.

1. Zechariah prophesied about the same time as _____.

2. Most scholars think that the last six chapters were written _____than the first eight.

3. Zechariah describes _____and _____them.

Answers: 1. Haggai; 2. later; 3. visions, interprets

113 REPENTANCE AND PROMISE (chapter 14)

Read Hosea 14.

1. What does Hosea urge Israel to do?

2. When the people of Israel give up their idols, the Lord will be a source of what to them?

NOTE: Verse 9 may have been added during or after the exile by a reader schooled in Hebrew wisdom who, seeing the fulfillment of Hosea's prophecies, commends the book to the wise of every generation.

```
H    1. Hosea's Marriage: A      8th
O        Living Parable           c
S                                 e
E    2. Israel's Crimes and       n
A        Punishment               t
                                  u
     3. Repentance and            r
         Promise                  y
                                 B.C.
```

* * * * * * * * * * * * * *

213B   Historical Note: Amos and Amaziah

Read Amos 7:10-17.

1. What report did Amaziah, priest of Bethel, send to Jeroboam?

2. How did Amos reply to Amaziah's command to go back to Judah?

* * * * * * * * * * * * * *

320   INTRODUCTION TO NAHUM

Nahum wrote this poem to celebrate the fall of Nineveh, Assyria in 612 B.C. This event meant freedom for Israel from its evil enemy. Nahum was a contemporary of Jeremiah, but, unlike Jeremiah, he was a prophet of good news. The oracles may have been written for use in public worship. An acrostic psalm of praise (A – K) introduces the book.

* * * * * * * * * * * * * *

421   PROPHECIES FROM THE TIME OF ZERUBBABEL (chapters 1--8)

Read Zechariah 1--3.

1. Note the first three visions. The one of the horns and workers refers to the overthrow of nations that opposed Judah. To what do the horses and the measuring line refer?

2. When Satan was condemned for accusing Joshua, how did the angel describe Joshua?

3. In the vision of the High Priest, what did the angel say his servant would be called?

4. What was the meaning of the seven-faceted stone?

```
Z    1. Prophecies from     6th
E        the Time of         c
C        Zerubbabel          e
H                            n
A                            t
R                            u
I                            r
A                            y
H                           B.C.
```

113

1. To return to the Lord; to pray for forgiveness

2. The source of all their blessings

* * * * * * * * * * * * * *

213B

1. "Amos is plotting against you."

2. Amos was not a paid prophet, but was obeying the Lord. The Lord would destroy Amaziah, his family, and his nation.

* * * * * * * * * * * * * *

320   INTRODUCTION TO NAHUM

Complete the following statements and then check the answers upside down.

1. The purpose of this poem is to _____ the _____ of _____.

2. Although living about the time of Jeremiah, Nahum wrote _____ news, not _____.

3. The oracles may have been used in _____ _____.

Answers: 1. celebrate, fall, Nineveh; 2. good, bad; 3. public worship

* * * * * * * * * * * * * *

421

1. The restoration of Jerusalem

2. "A stick snatched from the fire"

3. The Branch (This seems to refer to Zerubbabel who was thought to be the Messiah.)

4. The Lord would remove Israel's sin in a single day.

Overthrow of enemies

Restoration of Jerusalem

JUST FOR FUN!   Hosea: Hidden Idols

The RSV translates Hosea 13:2 "Men kiss calves" while the TEV says "Men kiss...idols--idols in the shape of bulls." The gold calves that were intended to be God's footstools were worshiped instead of God! In every age people have worshiped things intended to serve them. See if you can find an idol hidden in each sentence on the next page.

Example: Watch this taxi do lots of tricks! (idol)

Idols for the 1980s and '90s are: (a) intellectual power; (b) sensual pleasure; (c) political power; (d) business success; (e) material comfort; (f) financial gain.

Turn to the next page for these idols hidden in sentences.

* * * * * * * * * * * * * *

213C Basket of Fruit and Altar
      Read Amos 8:1--9:10.

1. What did the basket of fruit mean?

2. Amos next saw a vision of the Lord standing beside the altar. To punish Israel for its unjustice and its idolatry, what did the Lord say he would do to the Temple?

213D Postscript: Future Restoration
      Read Amos 9:11-15.

After the Lord has punished Israel, where will he bring the people?

* * * * * * * * * * * * * *

321 JUDGMENT ON NINEVEH (chapter 1)
     Read Nahum 1.

1. What great crime did the leader from Nineveh commit?

2. What good news did the messenger bring?

322 THE FALL OF NINEVEH (chapters 2--3)
     Read Nahum 2--3.

Who claims to be Nineveh's enemy?

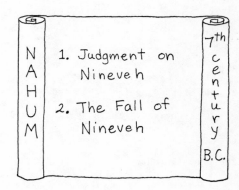

* * * * * * * * * * * * * *

421 PROPHECIES FROM THE TIME OF ZERUBBABEL (*continued*)
     Read Zechariah 4; scan 5--8.

4. What represents the two men God chose and anointed to serve him?

5. What did God promise Zerubbabel?

After underlining the idol hidden in each sentence, check answers upside down at the end of the frame.

(See previous page for list of idols.)

1. Curb us in essentials and we will cuss U.C. cessions!

2. Iran's inflationary boom ate rials, while England's terrific O.M.* fortified the pound.

3. Those yells you take pride in tell E.C. Tua lots about you: "Help! Ow! Ernest attacks again!"

4. I have chosen Su, Al, and Tur. Will they hear my plea? Sure they will!

5. "Stiff! I!" Nanci always replies. "Just hear my saga in full!"

6. "Was the P.O. lit?" I called. "The P.O. we ran past just now?"

---

*Order of Merit

Answers: 1. (d); 2. (e); 3. (a); 4. (b); 5. (f); 6. (c)

Continue with 120 on the next page.

* * * * * * * * * * * * *

213C

1. "The end has come for my people Israel."

   (The Hebrew words "fruit" and "end" sound alike.)

2. He will tear it down.

213D

He will bring them back to their land.

4. Basket of fruit

5. Altar

The end

Back home!

People of Israel

* * * * * * * * * * * * *

321

1. He plotted against the Lord.

2. Nineveh fell. The Assyrians would never invade Judah again.

322

The Lord Almighty

JUDAH   Assyria

Never again !

* * * * * * * * * * * * *

421

4. The two olive trees on either side of the lampstand.

5. He would succeed in rebuilding the Temple through the strength of the Lord's spirit.

The opening verse of Joel gives no historical setting for the book, so it cannot be dated exactly. However, it appears to have been written long after the exile, in the 5th or 4th century B.C. during the reign of the Persians. Joel wrote to interpret the plague of locusts as a sign of the Day of the Lord. His book is remembered most often for God's promise to send his spirit upon all people just before the Day of the Lord, the prophecy that Peter claimed was fulfilled at Pentecost (Acts 2:17).

* * * * * * * * * * * * *

220 INTRODUCTION TO OBADIAH

Although the book of Obadiah is undated, it was probably written after the fall of Jerusalem in the 6th or 5th century B.C. Several of its first fourteen verses appear in Jeremiah 49. Nothing is known of Obadiah, other than this judgment he makes in the Lord's name.

The Edomites were the descendants of Esau, the brother of Jacob. Like Jeremiah, Obadiah accuses Edom of being deceived by her pride. Edom was especially condemned for having taken advantage of Judah after the fall of Jerusalem. Obadiah spoke of the tables being turned on the Day of the Lord.

* * * * * * * * * * * * *

330 INTRODUCTION TO HABAKKUK

Habakkuk (sounds like "tobacco") lived about the time of Nahum, near the end of the seventh century B.C. He was greatly troubled to see power in the hands of violent people who oppressed and abused those more righteous than they. This was probably written when the Babylonians were in power. Habakkuk was the first prophet to demand that God give a reason for his actions. The prophet receives his answer and praises God in terms of lasting faith.

* * * * * * * * * * * * *

422 THE MESSIAH AND FUTURE DELIVERANCE (chapters 9—14)

Read Zechariah 9; scan 10; read 11—13; scan 14.

NOTE: Although tradition attributes the entire book to Zechariah, critical scholars believe chapters 9—14 are from a different time. Some scholars think these chapters were written before the exile, but most think they were written at a later time, because of the reference to Greece in 9:13. They describe the messianic age. The New Testament frequently refers to these passages.

ZECHARIAH

1. Prophecies from the Time of Zerubbabel

2. The Messiah and Future Deliverance

6th century B.C.

1. Why should the people of Zion rejoice?

2. What did the two shepherds represent—the one who looked after the sheep and the worthless one?

3   When will the sheep be scattered, many attacked by the Lord and killed?

4. What will the Lord do for those who remain?

120   INTRODUCTION TO JOEL

Circle the letter of the ONE BEST answer for each question.   Then check your answers upside down below.

1. Joel probably lived during the:
    a. Assyrian Empire
    b. Exile from Jerusalem
    c. Persian Empire
    d. Maccabean rule
    e. Roman rule

2. Joel saw the plague of locusts as a sign of:
    a. The coming Day of the Lord
    b. God's wrath poured out on the priests
    c. God's abandonment of Israel
    d. The invasion of Assyria
    e. b and c

3. Joel is best known for this prophecy:
    a. Darkness and gloom for Israel
    b. God's spirit poured out on all
    c. Devastation of the whole earth
    d. The return of the exiles to Jerusalem
    e. a and c

Answers: 1. c; 2. a; 3. b

* * * * * * * * * * * * * * *

220   INTRODUCTION TO OBADIAH

Complete the following statements.   Then check your answers upside down at the end of the frame.

1. The purpose of this book is to announce judgment upon _____.

2. The Edomites were descendants of _____.

3. Edomites were mean to the people of Judah at the time of _____'s _____.

4. The tables will be turned on the _____ of the _____.

Answers: 1. Edom; 2. Esau; 3. Jerusalem's fall; 4. Day, Lord

* * * * * * * * * * * * * * *

330   INTRODUCTION TO HABAKKUK

Complete the following statements.   Then check your answers upside down at the end of the frame.

1. He lived near the end of the _____century B.C.

2. Habakkuk's main concern was the power of _____ _____people over those more _____ than themselves.

3. Habakkuk probably lived at the time of the _____Empire.

Answers: 1. seventh; 2. violent, righteous; 3. Babylonian

* * * * * * * * * * * * * * *

422

1. Their king is coming (humble and riding on a donkey).

NOTE: This passage is quoted in the account of Jesus' entry to
       Jerusalem, Matthew 21:5 and John 12:15.

2. The good leader and the wicked one

NOTE: The thirty pieces of silver, the sum they thought the good
       shepherd was worth, are alluded to in Matthew 26, verse 15.
       Also, Jesus quotes the part about the sheep scattering when
       the shepherd is killed in Matthew 26:31 and Mark 14:27.

3. When God kills the good shepherd (see Zech. 11:4 and 13:7)

4. He will purify them. When they pray he will answer, "They are
    my people ... I am their God."

121　THE PLAGUE OF LOCUSTS (chapters 1:1--2:17)

Read Joel 1.

1. What had attacked the land?
2. Why were each of these groups--wine-drinkers, priests, and farmers--unhappy?
3. How did Joel describe the Day of the Lord?

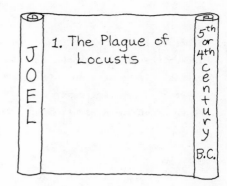

* * * * * * * * * * * *

221　THE PUNISHMENT OF EDOM (verses 1-14)

Read Obadiah 1-14.

1. "Your pride has deceived you" (verse 3). The Edomites thought that they were protected from attack. Why did they think that they were safe?
2. What terrible crime did Edom commit?

222　THE DAY OF THE LORD (verses 15-21)

Read Obadiah 15-21.

1. When the Lord judges all nations, who will rule Edom?
2. Who will be king?

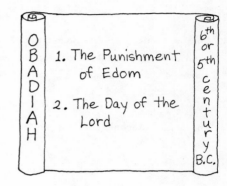

* * * * * * * * * * * *

331　HABAKKUK'S DIALOGUE WITH GOD (chapters 1:1--2:4)

Read Habakkuk 1:1--2:4.

1. What injustice does Habakkuk protest in this prayer for help?
2. What is the Lord's answer?

332　DOOM ON THE UNRIGHTEOUS (chapter 2:5-20)

Read Habakkuk 2:5-20.

Who is doomed?

NOTE:　Habakkuk 2:14 is found in the hymn "God Is Working His Purpose Out," and verse 20 is often used as a call to worship.

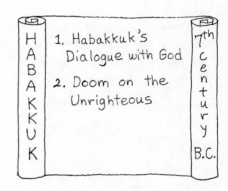

* * * * * * * * * * * *

JUST FOR FUN!　　　　Zechariah:　Messianic Prophecies

```
N S A D I V A D E M
A O R O V A F B E T
I S D E S N P R L O
T H I R T Y R A B F
N E M O E L I N M O
U E P K Y H E C U L
O P N T I R P H H I
F O I F A N L E S V
D N O I Z N G O H E
U T E D R E V L I S
```

In the puzzle at the left, can you find these words associated with messianic prophecies in Zechariah? They are spelled both forwards and backwards and appear in vertical, horizontal, or diagonal positions.

KING (Zec. 9:9)
DONKEY (Zec. 9:9)
UNITY (Zec. 11:7)
SILVER (Zec. 11:12)
THIRTY (Zec. 11:12)
FAVOR (Zec. 11:7)
ZION (Zec. 9:9)
SHEEP (Zec. 13:7)

HUMBLE (Zec. 9:9)
DAVID (Zec. 12:8; 13:1)
SHELTERS (Zec. 14:18)
FOUNTAIN (Zec. 13:1)
BRANCH (Zec. 3:8; 6:12)
MT OF OLIVES (Zec. 14:4)
SHEPHERD (Zec. 11:4; 13:7)

Turn to the next page for answers.

121

1. Hordes of locusts
2. Wine-drinkers: The grapes were destroyed.

   Priests: There were no offerings for the Temple.

   Farmers: Crops were destroyed.
3. The day when the Almighty brings destruction

* * * * * * * * * * * *

221

1. They were high in the mountains.
2. When Jerusalem fell, Edom looted the city and handed over
   those who were escaping to their enemies.

222

1. The men of Jerusalem
2. The Lord

* * * * * * * * * * * *

331

1. Evil men get the better of those more righteous than they.
2. "The time is coming quickly .... Those who are evil will not
   survive, but those who are righteous will live because they
   are faithful to God."

332

The conquerors, the wicked

* * * * * * * * * * * *

JUST FOR FUN! Answer

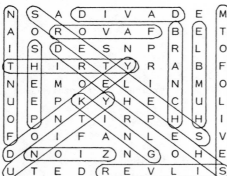

Haggai: Two Temples or Three?

Mount Moriah was the site of three major Temple-building
projects. Haggai urged the Jews to build the Second Temple
(Zerubbabel's). The most modest of the three, it had the
longest life, 495 years. It was known by four or perhaps five
of the prophets. Most of the prophets knew the first Temple,
Solomon's, which lasted 373 years. In 19 B.C. Herod started
expansions so vast that the renovated Second Temple was called
"Herod's Temple." Only the New Testament prophets knew this
third and most magnificent Temple, which lasted only 89 years.
Just for fun check the Chronology of the Bible in the back of
your *Good News Bible* (TEV) for the prophets who knew each
Temple. (First: 959-586 B.C.; Second: 515-20 B.C.;
Third: 19 B.C.-A.D. 70.)

121   THE PLAGUE OF LOCUSTS *(continued)*
      Read Joel 2:1-17.

4. What is the plague of locusts like?

5. What does the Lord want the people to do instead of just tearing their clothes?

* * * * * * * * * * * * * *

230   INTRODUCTION TO JONAH

Jonah is a story about a prophet who did not want to obey God. The story is set in the time of the Assyrian Empire, the great enemy of Israel. Tradition has held the eighth or seventh century as the date of writing, while most modern scholars conclude that it was written after the return to Jerusalem. Many of these scholars believe it was written to counter, with a prophetic view, the narrow exclusivism of post-exilic Judaism in the 5th or 4th centuries B.C. Certainly the book teaches that God has great compassion and love for all people. Rather than a God of wrath, who destroys the wicked, God is shown at work bringing people back to himself, even those who attack his people Israel.

* * * * * * * * * * * * * *

333   HABAKKUK'S PRAYER (chapter 3)
      Read Habakkuk 3.

1. Habakkuk praises God in this beautiful psalm. What fills the prophet with awe?

2. The prophet's faith is lasting. Can you give two of the four reasons why the prophet will still be joyful while waiting for God's time?

HABAKKUK
1. Habakkuk's Dialogue with God
2. Doom on the Unrighteous
3. Habakkuk's Prayer
7th century B.C.

* * * * * * * * * * * * * *

430   INTRODUCTION TO MALACHI

Malachi was written in the fifth century B.C., so the Temple had been rebuilt years before. "Malachi" means "my messenger." The main concern in Malachi was to urge renewal of faithfulness to the people's covenant with God. After protesting the breaking of marriage vows and the nonpayment of tithes, Malachi speaks of the future, identifying the messenger who prepares the way for the Messiah as Elijah.

4. Fire, an army

5. To repent with broken hearts and return to God with fasting and mourning

NOTE: The King James Version reads "Rend your hearts and not your garments."

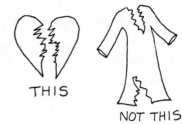

THIS

NOT THIS

* * * * * * * * * * * * * *

230   INTRODUCTION TO JONAH

Complete the following statements.   Then check answers upside down at the end of the frame.

1. This story is set in the time of the _____ Empire of the 8th-7th century B.C.

2. Jonah did not want to _____ God.

3. Most contemporary scholarship dates Jonah as written after the _____ to _____.

Answers: 1. Assyrian; 2. obey; 3. return, Jerusalem

* * * * * * * * * * * * * *

333

1. The things he has heard that the Lord has done

2. The Lord is my savior.
    He gives me strength.
    He makes me sure-footed.
    He keeps me safe on the mountains.

You brought victory to your people.... I will....wait... still...joyful....

* * * * * * * * * * * * * *

430   INTRODUCTION TO MALACHI

Circle the letter of the ONE BEST answer for each, and complete the statements.   Then check answers upside down at the end of the   frame.

1. Malachi was written about:
    a. 650 B.C.
    b. 550 B.C.
    c. 450 B.C.
    d. 350 B.C.

2. The major concern of Malachi was:
    a. Covenant renewal
    b. A new covenant with God
    c. Warning of coming judgment
    d. Announcement of the Messiah

3. Malachi means _____ _____

4. Malachi is remembered for predicting the return of _____.

Answers: 1. c; 2. a; 3. my messenger; 4. Elijah

122   PROMISE OF RESTORATION (chapter 2:18-27)

Read Joel 2:18-27.

1. What is the Lord going to give his people?
2. What will God do that will lead Israel to praise the Lord?

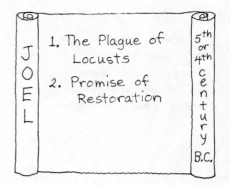

* * * * * * * * * * * * *

231   JONAH DISOBEYS THE LORD (chapter 1)

Read Jonah 1.

1. When God told Jonah to speak against Nineveh, what did Jonah do?
2. What happened to Jonah after he told the sailors he was the reason God had sent the storm?

232   JONAH'S PRAYER (chapter 2)

Read Jonah 2.

When Jonah thanked God for answering his prayer and praised God saying, "Salvation is from the Lord," what did God order?

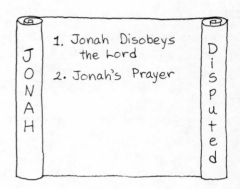

* * * * * * * * * * * * *

340   INTRODUCTION TO ZEPHANIAH

A prophet in Judah, Zephaniah lived in the seventh century B.C., probably just before King Josiah's reforms and Jeremiah's ministry. He called sin a crime against God and, like other prophets, he preached punishment for idolatry in Judah and other nations as well. Predicting the restoration of Jerusalem, Zephaniah "saw" it inhabited by those God had changed into a humble and righteous people. He also predicted the conversion of the nations after he had punished them. (See Zep. 2:11; 3:9; also Is. 56 and Zec. 14:9, 16.)

* * * * * * * * * * * * *

431   ISRAEL'S SINS (chapters 1:1--2:16)

Read Malachi 1:1--2:16.

1. The Lord has devastated Edom, Esau's hill country, the enemy of Israel. What does Malachi say that this shows?
2. In what two ways have the priests broken their covenant with God?
3. How did the people of Judah despise the covenant?

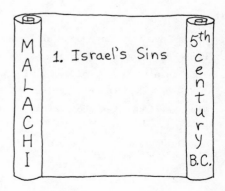

122

1. Grain, wine, and olive oil
2. Any one of these will do:
   God will give them back what they lost to the locusts.
   They will have plenty to eat and be satisfied.
   God has done wonderful things for them.
   They will never be despised.

* * * * * * * * * * * * * *

231

1. He sailed for Spain to get away from the Lord.
2. He was thrown into the sea to calm it down, was swallowed by a large fish, and lived inside it three days.

232

God ordered the fish to spit up Jonah on the beach.

* * * * * * * * * * * * *

340   INTRODUCTION TO ZEPHANIAH

Complete the following blanks. Then check the answers upside down at the end of the frame.

1. Zephaniah lived in the _____ century B.C.
2. He saw _____ as a _____ against God.
3. Zephaniah predicted the _____ of Jerusalem.
4. He prophesied that God would make the people _____ and _____.

Answers: 1. 7th; 2. sin, crime; 3. restoration; 4. humble, righteous

* * * * * * * * * * * * *

431

1. God's love for the people of Israel. (His choice of Jacob's descendants over Esau's.)
2. They cheated God by offering sick or stolen animals and worthless food; and their teaching led many to do wrong.
3. They married wives who worshiped idols and they broke their marriage vows.

123 THE DAY OF THE LORD (chapters 2:28--3:21)

Read Joel 2:28--3:21.

NOTE: Joel 2:28-32 is quoted by Peter in Acts 2:17-21.

1. Just before the Day of the Lord comes, what will the Lord pour upon all people?

2. Who will be saved from the terrible destruction when God judges the nations?

NOTE: Joel 3:10 is also found in Isaiah 2:4 and Micah 4:3, but in reverse--"swords into plows."

3. What is to be announced to the nations?

4. When the Lord roars from Mt. Zion, how will he treat his people?

JUST FOR FUN memorize the well-known verses 28-29 of chapter 2, which are quoted in Acts 2:17-18.

* * * * * * * * * * * *

JOEL
1. The Plague of Locusts
2. Promise of Restoration
3. The Day of the Lord
5th or 4th century B.C.

233 JONAH OBEYS THE LORD (chapter 3)

Read Jonah 3.

1. When Jonah told the people of Nineveh that their city would be destroyed in 40 days, how did they show that they believed in God?

2. What did God do then?

* * * * * * * * * * * *

JONAH
1. Jonah Disobeys the Lord
2. Jonah's Prayer
3. Jonah Obeys the Lord
Disputed

341 THE DAY OF THE LORD (chapters 1:1--2:3)

Read Zephaniah 1:1--2:3.

NOTE: Zephaniah 1:14-18 inspired Joel's description of the Day of the Lord, as well as the opening words of the medieval hymn, "Dies Irae" (O Day of Wrath...).

The Lord will punish all nations to teach them. What does Zephaniah tell the people of Judah to do?

342 DOOM OF ISRAEL'S NEIGHBORS (chapter 2:4-15)

Read Zephaniah 2:4-15.

After God punishes the nations and wipes out their gods, what will the nations do?

* * * * * * * * * * * *

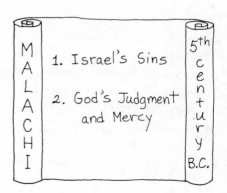

ZEPHANIAH
1. The Day of the Lord
2. Doom of Israel's Neighbors
7th century B.C.

432 GOD'S JUDGMENT AND MERCY (chapters 2:17--4:6)

Read Malachi 2:17--4:6.

1. "I will send my messenger to prepare the way for me." What image is used to represent the messenger as judge?

2. "I am the Lord, and I do not change." How are the people cheating God?

3. God promises justice on the Day of the Lord. What will happen to those who obey God?

4. Malachi concludes with a note about Moses and Elijah. When will God send Elijah?

MALACHI
1. Israel's Sins
2. God's Judgment and Mercy
5th century B.C.

123

1. He will pour out his spirit.
2. All who ask the Lord for help
3. "Prepare for war.... Hammer the points of your plows into swords."
4. He will defend them.

* * * * * * * * * * * * *

233

1. They and their animals fasted and put on sackcloth and ashes; they prayed and gave up evil actions.
2. He changed his mind and did not punish them.

* * * * * * * * * * * * *

341

He tells them to obey the Lord: "Do what is right, and humble yourselves before the Lord."

342

They will worship him in their own lands.

* * * * * * * * * * * * *

432

1. Strong soap and fire to refine metal
2. They are not paying their tithes.
3. "My saving power will rise on you like the sun and bring healing like the sun's rays."
4. Before the Day of the Lord

NOTE: This verse led many to expect Elijah to return before the Messiah appeared.

JUST FOR FUN!

Unscramble the letters of each word from Joel and write the correct words in the squares. (The verse of Joel in which each appears is given.) Then use the letters that fall in the squares with circles inside to unscramble the words in the phrase that gives God's promise. Write these words in the squares below.

CLUE: What God promises to do

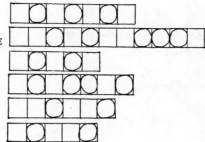

Joel: God's Promise

Joel 1:4	SCLUTOS
Joel 1:15	STORTIDUNCE
Joel 1:11	SCORP
Joel 2:28	SNOIVIS
Joel 2:12	PERTEN
Joel 3:1	DAJUH

Turn to the next page for the answer.

* * * * * * * * * * * * *

234   JONAH'S ANGER AND GOD'S MERCY (chapter 4)

   Read Jonah 4.

1. Why was Jonah angry?
2. What did God teach Jonah through the creation and death of the plant?

J
O
N
A
H

1. Jonah Disobeys the Lord
2. Jonah's Prayer
3. Jonah Obeys the Lord
4. Jonah's Anger and God's Mercy

D
i
s
p
u
t
e
d

* * * * * * * * * * * * *

343   JERUSALEM'S DOOM AND REDEMPTION (chapter 3)

   Read Zephaniah 3.

1. What does God say he will do to the people of the nations after he punishes them?
2. After Israel has been punished, what changes will God make in Israel for those who survive?
3. Why does Jerusalem no longer need to be afraid?

NOTE: A song of joy closes the book.

Z
E
P
H
A
N
I
A
H

1. The Day of the Lord
2. Doom of Israel's Neighbors
3. Jerusalem's Doom and Redemption

7th century B.C.

* * * * * * * * * * * * *

JUST FOR FUN!   Prophet Acrostics

Here are sample acrostics for the prophets in this section. Try your hand at writing verbal portraits of each of The Twelve (spelling the name of each prophet vertically).

M y messenger (Mal. 3:1)
A ltars of worthless food (1:7)
L ord's love for Israel (1:2)
A bundance of good things for faithful givers (3:10)
C heaters: Priests and people (1:14; 3:8)
H onor me in your marriages (2:11, 14)
I will send Elijah (4:5)

H ouses for themselves, God's house in ruins (1:4)
A lways be with you--my promise (1:13; 2:5)
G rain ruined by hail (no repentance) (2:16, 17)
G overnor to rule in God's name (2:23)
A ll the people obeyed God and worked on Temple (1:14)
I will bless you (2:19)

Continue the JUST FOR FUN on the next page.

JUST FOR FUN!   Joel: God's Promise

Answer: TO POUR OUT HIS SPIRIT (Joel 2:28)

Just for fun, look up these verses from Joel that are mentioned in Revelation, often with their ideas developed even further.

Joel	Revelation
1:6 and 2:4-5	9:3-9
2:10	8:12
2:11	6:17
3:13	14:15, 19, 20

You may also be interested in noting that Joel 2:31 is described in all three synoptic Gospels.

Study the outlines of Hosea and Joel on page 96 and their section charts on page 121.   Then take Section Test 1 on page 125.

* * * * * * * * * * * * *

234

1. God had spared his enemy, Nineveh.
2. The reason why God has compassion for all people

Study the outlines of Amos, Obadiah, and Jonah on page 96 and their section charts on page 122.   Then take Section Test 2 on page 126.

* * * * * * * * * * * * *

343

1. He will change them so that they will pray to him alone and will obey him.
2. They will do no wrong and will be prosperous, joyful, and victorious.
3. God has stopped their punishment, removed their enemies, and given them victory and new life.

JERUSALEM:

Punishment   Victory
Enemies   New life

Study the outlines and section charts of Micah, Nahum, Habakkuk, and Zephaniah on pages 96 and 123. Then take Section Test 3 on page 127.

* * * * * * * * * * * * *

JUST FOR FUN!   Prophet Acrostics

Z erubbabel, The Branch (Zec. 3:8; 6:12)
E recting the Second Temple (1:16; 4:7-9)
C oming of the King (9:9)
H igh Priest honored (3:1--4:5, 10b-14)
A ngels (1--6)
R estoration of Jerusalem (1:16; 2:4, 12; 8:3-5)
I nsincerity and disobedience condemned (7)
A pocalyptic approach (13--14)
H oly city purified (13:1-2, 9)

Studying these and any other prophet acrostics that you may write will reinforce summaries of the themes and content for each prophet.

Study the outlines and section charts for Haggai, Zechariah, and Malachi on pages 96 and 124 before taking Section Test 4 on page 128.

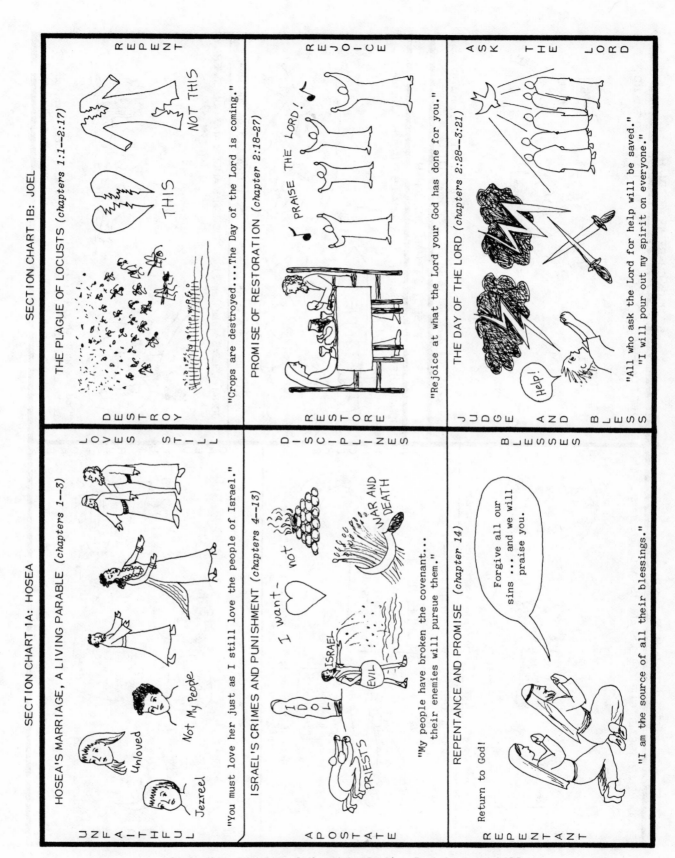

Study these charts and then take Section Test 1 on page 125.

THE DAY OF THE LORD
(verses 15-21)

LORD

MEN OF JERUSALEM

EDOM

"Because you killed your brothers,
you will be destroyed."

THE PUNISHMENT OF EDOM
(verses 1-14)

Gloats
Loots

EDOM

"Your pride has deceived you."

SECTION CHART 2C: JONAH

JONAH'S PRAYER (chapter 2)

"Salvation is from the Lord."

JONAH DISOBEYS (chapter 1)

NINEVEH
NO!

"The sea ... calmed down at once."

JONAH'S ANGER AND GOD'S MERCY
(chapter 4)

I told you!

"How much more, then, should
I have pity on Nineveh!"

JONAH OBEYS (chapter 3)

GOD WILL PUNISH YOU!

"God saw what they did....
So he changed his mind and
did not punish them."

SECTION CHART 2A: AMOS

JUDGMENT: ISRAEL'S NEIGHBORS AND ISRAEL (chapters 1—2)

U N J U S T

Prophets

people

you have sinned!

"So I will send fire."

"The people of _____ have sinned again and again."

J U D G E

WARNINGS TO ISRAEL (chapters 3—6)

I N S I N C E R E

CONDEMNED
Life of Rich!
Irresponsible!

ISRAEL

NATIONS

JUSTICE

"Hate what is evil; love what is right."
"Let justice flow like a stream."

P U N I S H

FIVE VISIONS (chapters 7—9)

D O O M E D

B U T

R E S T O R E D

4. Basket of fruit
5. Altar

Jeroboam;
Amos plots
against you.
Amaziah

Amos,
go home!

Stop Lord!

1. Locusts
2. Fire

3. Plumb line

"Afterward: I will restore the kingdom of David."

P U N I S H   A N D   R E S T O R E

Study these charts. Then take Section Test 2 on page 126.

Study these charts. Then take Section Test 3 on page 127.

SECTION CHART 4B: ZECHARIAH

RESTORATION

PROPHECIES FROM THE TIME OF ZERUBBABEL *(chapters 1—8)*

Beautiful!

The Branch

The two anointed ones

"You will succeed by my spirit."

VISION

KING AND APOCALYPSE

MESSIAH AND FUTURE DELIVERANCE *(chapters 9—14)*

Mount of Olives

Victorious but humble

PURIFY

Fire

Fountain

"They paid me thirty pieces of silver as my wages."

MESSAGES

SECTION CHART 4A: HAGGAI

REBUILD THE TEMPLE *(chapters 1:1—2:19)*

GOD

SELF

More splendid than the old

Reason for unsuccessful lives

PROMISE TO ZERUBBABEL *(chapter 2:20—23)*

ZERUBBABEL

In God's name

"You are the one I have chosen."

Powers overthrown

SECTION CHART 4C: MALACHI

ISRAEL'S SINS *(chapters 1:1—2:16)*

I take this woman

GOD

"You must honor me by what you do."

Cheaters!

GOD'S JUDGMENT AND MERCY *(chapters 2:17—4:6)*

I will send Elijah!

Healing

10% to GOD

Cheaters!

"I will send my messenger to prepare the way for me."

Study these charts and then take Section Test 4 on page 128.

SECTION TEST 1: HOSEA AND JOEL

A. STRUCTURE

Outline. Complete the following:

HOSEA

1. _____'s _____, a _____
    _____

2. _____'s _____ and _____

3. _____ and _____

JOEL

4. The _____ of _____

5. _____ of _____

6. The _____ of the _____

C. PROPHECY

Signs and Visions. Write the number of the sign or
vision before its ONE meaning.

1. Jezreel

2. Unloved

3. Gomer

4. Hosea's marriage

5. Half-baked loaf

6. Silly pigeon

7. Not-My-People

8. Plague of locusts

____ Israel's going to many
     nations for help

____ God's rejection of a
     sinful Israel

____ God's aversion to the
     sins of Israel

____ Reliance on others
     weakened Israel

____ Son named to show end
     of Jehu's dynasty

____ The Day of the Lord will
     soon come

____ The relationship between
     God and Israel

____ Unfaithful Israel

About Prophecies. Circle the ONE BEST answer.

1. God told Hosea to treat his prostitute wife:

    a. With punishment decreed in his law
    b. By restraining her sinful actions
    c. With love as the Lord loves Israel
    d. By praising her

2. Instead of animal sacrifice, Hosea says the Lord
    wants:

    a. His people's constant love
    b. Obedience to his rule for worship
    c. His people's joy in life and work
    d. a and b

3. Hosea. Harnessed for harder work, Israel
    planted and harvested:

    a. Evil; war and death
    b. Righteousness; blessings
    c. Obedience; full life
    d. Laziness; trouble

4. Hosea. When Israel worships God alone, the
    Lord:

    a. Will make Israel a mighty nation
    b. Will be the source of all their blessings
    c. Will punish their enemies
    d. Will bring them home again

5. Joel says the Day of the Lord is the day:

    a. When God reveals himself fully
    b. When Israel is honored by all nations
    c. When the Lord brings destruction on the
        earth
    d. a and b

6. Joel. These will be saved from destruction:

    a. Those who call on the Lord's name
    b. Those who live a good life
    c. Those who obey the law of Moses
    d. Those who worship in the Temple

7. Joel. The nations are told to:

    a. Prepare for war
    b. Make plows out of swords
    c. Put an end to all fighting
    d. a and b

D. FEATURES

Background. Complete the following statements.

1. Hosea's _____ was a parable of God's
    _____ for Israel.

2. Hosea was a prophet in the _____
    _____ just before the fall of
    _____.

3. Joel probably lived during the _____
    Empire.

4. Joel wrote to interpret the _____
    of _____ as a sign of the
    _____ of the _____.

Quotations. Write H for Hosea or J for Joel to
show the source of each of these quotations.

1. ____ I am the source of all their blessings.

2. ____ All who ask the Lord for help will be
         saved.

3. ____ I will pour out my spirit on everyone.

4. ____ The people do not acknowledge me as God.

5. ____ Your old men will have dreams, and your
         young men will see visions.

6. ____ Called him out of Egypt as my son.

7. ____ How can I give you up, Israel?...My love
         for you is too strong.

8. ____ Hammer the points of your plows into
         swords.

*Check your answers on page 134. Compute your scores on page 137 and enter them on the Unit 3 growth record
on page 138. After studying any items missed, begin the study of Amos on page 97.*

125

SECTION TEST 2: AMOS, OBADIAH, AND JONAH

A. STRUCTURE

Complete the following outlines.

AMOS

1. _____: _____'s _____
   and _____.

2. _____ to _____

3. _____ _____

OBADIAH

4. The _____ of _____

5. The _____ of the _____

JONAH

6. _____ _____ the _____

7. _____'s _____

8. _____ _____ the _____

9. _____'s _____ and _____'s _____

C. PROPHECY

Write the number of the prophet, king, or place before the prophecy or other term with which it is most closely associated.

1. Tekoa	____ Pride due to living in the mountains
2. Bethel	____ Preached judgment on Edom
3. Edom	____ Ordered not to speak God's message
4. Prophets	____ Told the king Amos was plotting against him
5. Nineveh	____ Repented in sackcloth
6. Amaziah	____ Israel's king whose dynasty would be ended
7. Jonah	____ Amaziah's home where altars to be destroyed
8. Obadiah	____ Home of Amos
9. Jeroboam II	____ Ran away from God

Circle the ONE BEST answer for each prophecy.

10. The reason given for heavy judgment of Israel's sin was that:

    a. It was the only nation God chose and cared for.
    b. Israel had burned her children in sacrifice.
    c. God's law is righteous.
    d. b and c

11. Amos condemned the well-to-do because:

    a. They had no compassion for others.
    b. They felt no responsibility for the poor.
    c. They got rich by oppressing the poor.
    d. All of the above

12. When Amos prayed for Israel:

    a. The people repented.
    b. God restored the leaders of Israel.
    c. God relented about sending locusts and fire.
    d. Amos was transported to the Temple.

13. Obadiah condemns Edom for:

    a. Looting Jerusalem after its fall
    b. Handing escapees over to their enemy
    c. Killing the prophets sent from Judah
    d. a and b

14. The People of Nineveh repented in ashes:

    a. After Jonah preached judgment
    b. Because they believed God
    c. And then God did not punish them
    d. All of the above

D. FEATURES

Background. Complete these statements.

1. Amos stressed the need for _____ _____.

2. Amos lived _____ the fall of the _____ Kingdom.

3. Obadiah was written _____ the fall of Jerusalem.

4. The setting for Jonah is during the _____ Empire.

5. Jonah teaches God's _____ for _____ people.

Special Content. Write A for Amos, O for Obadiah, or J for Jonah before each item that distinguishes that book.

____ "Go to Nineveh and speak out against it."

____ "Let justice flow like a stream and righteousness like a river that never goes dry."

____ A large fish

____ Tables to be turned during the Day of the Lord

____ Plumb line and basket of fruit

Check your answers, page 134. Compute your scores, page 137, and enter them on Unit 3 growth record, page 138. After studying any items you missed, begin the study of Micah on page 97.

SECTION TEST 3: MICAH, NAHUM, HABAKKUK, AND ZEPHANIAH

A. STRUCTURE

Complete the following outline.

MICAH

1. _____ to _____ _____

2. _____ to _____:
   _____ and _____

NAHUM

3. _____ on _____

4. The _____ of _____

HABAKKUK

5. _____ 's _____ with _____

6. _____ on the _____

7. _____ 's _____

ZEPHANIAH

8. The _____ of the _____

9. _____ of _____ 's _____

10. _____ 's _____ and _____

C. PROPHECY

Write the number of the prophet or place before the ONE prophecy most closely associated with it.

1. Micah
2. Nahum
3. Habakkuk
4. Zephaniah
5. Bethlehem
6. Nineveh
7. Jerusalem
8. Assyria

____ Never again to invade Judah

____ Violent people oppress the righteous.

____ The Lord, their enemy

____ God's people who are humble and righteous will live there.

____ Birth of future ruler to ancient family line

____ The Day of the Lord is coming soon.

____ Prophet of good news

____ Evil men cheat the poor with false weights.

Circle the ONE BEST answer for each prophecy.

9. Micah accused these leaders of allowing their work to be influenced by those who paid them money:

   a. Priests
   b. Prophets
   c. Government leaders
   d. a, b, and c

10. Nahum condemned for making plans against God:

    a. The leader from Nineveh
    b. The people of Assyria
    c. The people of Judah
    d. The king of Judah

11. Habakkuk is filled with awe because the Lord:

    a. Has destroyed Nineveh
    b. Sends news of victory over the mountains
    c. Has done great things for his people
    d. Makes the deer sure-footed

12. _Zephaniah._ When the Lord restores Jerusalem the people will be prosperous and unafraid, for:

    a. Their enemies have been removed.
    b. Their punishment will be over.
    c. God's power will give them victory.
    d. All of the above.

D. FEATURES

Background. Complete these statements.

1. Micah lived in the _____ century.

2. Micah sees the nations's _____ as mainly responsible for the coming _____.

3. Nahum's oracles may have been written for use in _____ _____.

4. Nahum, Habakkuk, and Zephaniah lived in the _____ century.

5. Zephaniah condemns Judah's _____.

Special Content. Write H for Habakkuk, N for Nahum, M for Micah, or Z for Zephaniah before each item.

____ The Lord is in his holy Temple. Let all the ...

____ I am your enemy!

____ They will hammer their swords into plows.

____ The evil hurt the righteous.

____ To do what is just, to show constant love ...

____ Do what is right and humble yourselves.

Check your answers on page 135. Then compute your scores, page 137, and enter them on the Unit 3 growth record on page 138. After studying any items you missed, begin the study of Haggai on page 97.

A. STRUCTURE

Complete these outlines.

HAGGAI

1. _____ the _____

2. The _____ to _____

ZECHARIAH

3. _____ from the _____

   of _____

4. The _____ and _____

   _____

MALACHI

5. _____'s _____

6. _____'s _____ and _____

B. NARRATIVE

Write the number of the person before the ONE term most closely associated with that person. Use one number twice.

1. Zerubbabel   ____ Prophet who urged rebuilding

2. Joshua   ____ Governor of Judah

3. Haggai   ____ My messenger

4. Zechariah   ____ High priest

5. Malachi   ____ Visions and messianic age

        ____ Builder of the Second Temple

C. PROPHECY

Signs and Visions. Write the number of the sign or vision before the ONE term most closely associated with it. One term will have two numbers.

1. Measuring line   ____ Future king of peace

2. The Branch   ____ Good and bad leaders

3. Two shepherds   ____ Zerubbabel (thought to be the Messiah)

4. Seven-faceted stone

5. Olive trees, lampstand   ____ Two anointed leaders

        ____ Rebuilding Jerusalem

6. King on donkey   ____ Israel's sins removed in one day

7. Horses

About Prophecies. Circle the letter of the ONE BEST answer for each prophecy.

1. Haggai. The people are unsuccessful in building new lives because:

   a. They have planted little grain.
   b. They have worked only for the Lord.
   c. They have left God's Temple in ruins.
   d. They have worshiped foreign gods.

2. Zechariah. God promised Zerubbabel that he would:

   a. Rebuild the Temple
   b. Be honored by all nations
   c. Be tested by destructive war
   d. Save Israel leading the army of the Lord

3. Malachi. The Lord's messenger will be like:

   a. Strong soap
   b. Fire that refines metal
   c. Oil that heals
   d. a and b

4. Malachi. Israel sinned in ALL of these ways EXCEPT:

   a. Men married wives who worshiped idols.
   b. Priests offered stolen animals in sacrifice.
   c. The people did not pay their tithes.
   d. Priests offered sacrifices to Milcom.

D. FEATURES

Background. Complete these statements.

1. Haggai and Zechariah prophesied about _____ B.C.

2. Haggai urged _____ of Temple and land.

3. Zechariah described the _____ age.

4. Malachi was written _____ the Temple was built.

5. The purpose of Malachi was to inspire people to _____ of the _____.

Special Content. Write H for Haggai, Z for Zechariah, or M for Malachi before EACH of these items.

____ Horns and workers

____ New Temple more splendid than the old

____ I will send you the prophet Elijah.

____ My saving power will rise on you like the sun and bring healing.

____ They paid me thirty pieces of silver as my wages.

Check your answers on page 135. Then compute your scores, page 137, and enter them on the Unit 3 growth record, page 138. Then study all outlines, page 96, and charts, pages 121-124, before taking Unit Test 3.

A.   STRUCTURE

HOSEA

1. _____'s _____, a _____ _____
2. _____'s _____ and _____
3. _____ and _____

JOEL

4. The _____ of _____
5. _____ of _____
6. The _____ of the _____

AMOS

7. _____: _____ s _____ and _____
8. _____ to _____
9. _____ _____

OBADIAH

10. _____ of _____
11. The _____ of the _____

JONAH

12. _____ _____ the _____
13. _____ 's _____
14. _____ the _____
15. _____ 's _____ and _____ 's _____

MICAH

16. _____ to all _____
17. _____ to _____ : _____ and _____

NAHUM

18. _____ on _____
19. The _____ of _____

HABAKKUK

20. _____ 's _____ with _____
21. _____ on the _____
22. _____ 's _____

ZEPHANIAH

23. The _____ of the _____
24. _____ of _____ 's _____
25. _____ 's _____ and _____

HAGGAI

26. _____ the _____
27. The _____ to _____

ZECHARIAH

28. _____ from the _____ of _____
29. The _____ and _____

MALACHI

30. _____ 's _____
31. _____ 's _____ and _____

B.   NARRATIVE

People and Places. Write the number of the person or place before the ONE term with which it is most closely associated.

1. Amaziah
2. Joshua
3. Haggai
4. Nahum
5. Jeroboam II
6. Zerubbabel
7. Tekoa
8. Bethel
9. Edom
10. Nineveh

____ Called Temple Builder
____ Urged the Temple be rebuilt
____ Told good news
____ High Priest who led the rebuilding
____ Told king Amos was plotting against him
____ King's dynasty to end
____ Altars to be destroyed
____ God sent unwilling prophet here.
____ Looted Jerusalem after it fell
____ Amos lived here.

C.   PROPHECY

Signs and Visions. Write the number of the sign or vision before the ONE term with which it is most closely associated.

1. Two shepherds
2. Silly pigeon
3. Gomer
4. King riding on a donkey
5. Measuring line
6. Half-baked loaf
7. Seven-faceted stone
8. Hosea's marriage
9. Plague of locusts
10. Locusts and fire
11. Olive trees by lampstand
12. Horns and workers

____ Israel's sins removed in one day
____ Israel's unfaithfulness
____ Restoration of Israel
____ Overthrow of Israel's enemies
____ Anointed leaders
____ Day of the Lord
____ Israel going from one nation to next for aid
____ A good leader, a bad one
____ Destruction of Israel (averted by prayer)
____ Israel robbed of strength
____ God's relationship with Israel
____ Future king of peace

About Prophecies. Circle the letter of the ONE BEST answer for each statement about prophecies.

1. Hosea. The offering God really wants is:
   a. His people's obedience to the Law
   b. His people's constant love
   c. Sacrifice as specified in Scripture
   d. Payment of tithes

2. Joel. Those saved from coming ruin are those:
   a. Who live a good life
   b. Who obey the Law of Moses
   c. Who worship in the Temple
   d. Who ask the Lord for help

3. Amos. God chose only Israel to be his people, so:
   a. God will punish Israel.
   b. God will bless Israel.
   c. Israel will always obey him.
   d. Israel is the leader of the nations.

4. <u>Obadiah</u>. Edom will be punished for:
   a. Plundering Jerusalem after it fell
   b. Refusing to listen to the prophet
   c. Turning escaping Jews over to their enemies
   d. a and c

5. <u>Jonah</u>. The people of Nineveh escaped punishment for ALL these reasons EXCEPT:
   a. They repented in sackcloth and ashes.
   b. They and their animals fasted.
   c. Jonah begged God to forgive them.
   d. Jonah preached judgment on Nineveh.

6. <u>Micah</u>. Their decisions were corrupted by bribes:
   a. City officials
   b. Temple priests
   c. Prophets
   d. a, b, and c

7. <u>Nahum</u>. The leader from Nineveh was condemned:
   a. For making plans against God
   b. For defiling the Temple
   c. For worshiping idols
   d. a, b, and c

8. <u>Habakkuk</u>. The Lord has:
   a. Done great things for his people
   b. Vented his wrath on the nations
   c. Promised that the righteous will live
   d. a and c

9. <u>Zephaniah</u>. God punished the nations, wanting:
   a. Them to stop oppressing his people
   b. Them to serve Israel
   c. His people to know he loves them
   d. Them to pray to him alone and obey him

10. <u>Haggai</u>. Because the Temple was left in ruins:
    a. The Samaritans became enemies of the Jews.
    b. God sent an epidemic of disease.
    c. Israel did not prosper.
    d. Israel began to turn to foreign gods.

11. <u>Zechariah</u>. God promised that Zerubbabel would:
    a. Be king over all people and rule forever
    b. Complete the Temple by God's spirit
    c. Restore Jerusalem to its former glory
    d. Lead Jews to victory over the nations

12. <u>Malachi</u>. ALL are true of Israel's sin EXCEPT:
    a. God's people sell the holy vessels.
    b. People are not paying their tithes.
    c. God's messenger will be like strong soap.
    d. Priests show contempt for God's altar.

D. FEATURES

<u>Background</u>. Complete the following statements:

1. Amos lived in Judah and preached _____ _____ to _____.

2. The story of Jonah is set in the time of the _____ Empire.

3. Haggai urged _____ the Temple.

4. Zechariah prophesied through _____ and spoke of a _____.

5. Malachi urged a _____ _____.

Write the number of the century B.C. before EACH of the following prophets to show approximately the time of his major prophesying. Either of two centuries can be given for Obadiah. (Scholars do not agree on times for Joel and Jonah.)

____ Hosea   ____ Micah

____ Obadiah   ____ Nahum

____ Habakkuk   ____ Zechariah

____ Zephaniah   ____ Haggai

____ Amos   ____ Malachi

<u>Special Content</u>. Write the name of the prophet before the quotation or other item of content that distinguishes that book from others of the Twelve.

1. _____ "Hammer the points of your plows into swords."

2. _____ The army of locusts is a sign of the Day of the Lord.

3. _____ A plumb line and basket of fruit

4. _____ "Evil men get the better of the righteous."

5. _____ "Before the great and terrible day of the Lord comes, I will send ... Elijah."

6. _____ "The Lord is in his holy Temple; let everyone on earth be silent in his presence."

7. _____ "What he requires of us is this: to do what is just, to show constant love, and to live in humble fellowship with our God."

8. _____ "How can I give you up, Israel? ... My love for you is too strong."

9. _____ "Let justice flow like a stream, and righteousness like a river."

10. _____ A large fish

11. _____ "Your king is coming ... victorious, but humble and riding on a donkey."

12. _____ "They paid me thirty pieces of silver as my wages."

13. _____ A poem of celebration

14. _____ "Do what is right, and humble yourselves before the Lord."

15. _____ "I ... called him out of Egypt as my son."

16. _____ "I will pour out my spirit on everyone."

17. _____ "I will send my messenger to prepare the way for me."

18. _____ "My saving power will rise on you like the sun and bring healing like the sun's rays."

19. _____ "My people, why should you be living in well-built houses while my Temple lies in ruins?"

20. _____ "They will hammer their swords into plows."

Check answers on page 135. Then compute scores on page 137 and enter on the Unit 3 growth record on page 138. Compute growth in each area of knowledge. Study any items you may have missed. Then you will have completed the fourth and last book in the Mastering Old Testament Facts series.

ANSWERS TO TESTS IN UNIT 1

NOTE: If one item is out of order in the <u>Sequence</u> category of section or unit tests, consider it only one error, even though your other items will have different numbers from the numbers listed.

<u>PRE-TEST</u> Unit 1 *(100 points)*

A. STRUCTURE *(17)*

<u>Outline</u> *(7)*

1. c	5. d
2. a	6. d
3. c	7. a
4. b	

<u>Sequence</u> *(10)*

5	2
10	8
4	1
6	7
9	3

B. NARRATIVE *(30)*

<u>Rulers</u> *(9)*		<u>Prophets</u> *(6)*	
5	1	6	5
9	7	4	1
8	4	2	3
3	2		
	6		

<u>Places</u> *(10)*		<u>Events</u> *(5)*
10	7	1. d
3	6	2. d
2	8	3. a
4	9	4. d
1	5	5. a

C. PROPHECY *(25)*

<u>Signs</u> *(15)*

2	15
6	12
1	13
3	11
7	9
5	14
4	10
8	

<u>About Prophecies</u> *(10)*

1. d	8
2. d	9
3. b	6
4. c	7
5. c	10

D. FEATURES *(28)*

<u>Background</u> *(8)*		<u>Special Content</u> *(7)*	
2	J	2	J, L
L	1	1	J, 1
1	3	1	1
J	2	2	

<u>Quotations</u> *(13)*

2	1	L
J	2	J
3	1	3
2	1	2
L		

<u>SECTION TEST 1</u> - Isaiah 1--25 *(50 points)*

A. STRUCTURE *(10)*

<u>Outline</u> *(6)*

1. Coming Judgment
2. Warnings; Promises
3. Judgment; Nations
4. Judgment; Earth
5. Warnings; Promises
6. Assyrian Threat

<u>Sequence</u> *(4)*

2
4
1
3

B. NARRATIVE *(13)*

<u>Persons</u> *(6)*

3	1
4	5
6	2

<u>Places</u> *(7)*

4	7
3	2
6	1
	5

C. PROPHECY *(12)*

<u>Signs</u> *(6)*

4	5
6	1
3	2

<u>About Prophecies</u> *(6)*

1. a	4. c
2. c	5. b
3. d	6. d

D. FEATURES *(15)*

<u>Background</u> *(4)*

1. b
2. d
3. a
4. c

<u>Special Content</u> *(11)*

2	12
3	14
6	16
8	19
10	20
11	

<u>SECTION TEST 2</u> - Isaiah 40--55 *(25 points)*

A. STRUCTURE *(4)*

1. Hope; Exiles
2. Prologue; Good News
3. Consolation; Israel
4. Conclusion; Invitation; Promise

B. NARRATIVE *(8)*

4	8
5	6
1	3
2	7

C. PROPHECY *(5)*

1. a
2. b
3. d
4. d
5. c

D. FEATURES *(8)*

<u>Background</u> *(3)*	<u>Quotations</u> *(5)*
1. exile	1
2. suffering servant	4
3. console (or encourage), acting, history	5
	7
	10

<u>SECTION TEST 3</u> - Isaiah 56--66 *(20 points)*

A. STRUCTURE *(7)*

<u>Outline</u> *(4)*	<u>Sequence</u> *(3)*
1. Strengthening; Faith; Returned	II
2. Warnings; Promises	III
3. Salvation Songs	I
4. Final Warnings; Promises	

C. PROPHECY *(4)*

1. d
2. d
3. b
4. a

D. FEATURES *(9)*

<u>Background</u> *(2)*	<u>Quotations</u> *(7)*	
1. return, exiles (remnant, Jews)	1	8
2. reassure (encourage); religious; ethical	2	9
	5	11
	7	

<u>SECTION TEST 4</u> - Jeremiah 1--25 *(25 points)*

A. STRUCTURE *(5)*

<u>Outline</u> *(2)*

1. Jeremiah's Call
2. Prophecies; Reigns; Judah's Last Four Kings

<u>Sequence</u> *(3)*

3, 2, 1

B. NARRATIVE *(5)*

4	3
2	5
1	

C. PROPHECY *(10)*

<u>About Prophecies</u> *(4)*		<u>Signs</u> *(6)*	
1. d	3. b	4	3
2. c	4. a	5	1
		2	6

D. FEATURES *(5)*

<u>Background</u> *(2)*	<u>Quotations</u> *(3)*
1. Doom	1
2. Six	3
	4

SECTION TEST 5 – Jeremiah 26--52 and Lamentations
(50 points)

A. STRUCTURE (8)

Outline (4)   Sequence (4)

1. Events; Jeremiah's Life   1
2. Prophecies; Nations   4
3. Fall; Jerusalem   3
4. Five   2

B. NARRATIVE (19)

Persons and Places (10)   Events (9)

8   1   1. b   6. c
2   6   2. c   7. c
5   10   3. b   8. d
3   4   4. b   9. a
9   7   5. a

C. PROPHECY (11)

Signs (4)   About Prophecies (7)

4   1. b   5. b
1   2. d   6. c
3   3. d   7. a
2   4. a

D. FEATURES (12)

Background (5)   Quotations (7)

1. doom; changed; repentance   1. J   9. L
2. commemoration   2. L   10. J
3. fall; Jerusalem   4. J   12. J
4. sin   6. L
5. approval

UNIT TEST 1 (100 points)

(Pages and Scripture references for review are
given in parentheses.)

A. STRUCTURE (20)

Outline (9) (See page 10.)

1. Coming Judgment
2. Hope; Exiles
3. Strengthening; Faith; Return
4. Jeremiah's Call
5. Prophecies; Reigns; Judah's Last Four Kings
6. Events; Jeremiah's Life
7. Prophecies; Nations
8. Fall; Jerusalem
9. Five

Sequence (11)

6 (Jer. 34:8-11)   11 (Is. 56:8)
3 (Is. 37:36)   9 (Jer. 44)
1 (Is. 6)   8 (Jer. 39:1-10)
4 (Is. 39:2)   10 (Is. 45:13)
5 (Jer. 22:24-25)   7 (Jer. 37:11)
2 (Is. 7:1-2)

UNIT TEST 1 (continued)

B. NARRATIVE (25)

Persons and Places (20)

10 (Jer. 39:6-7)   16 (Jer. 7:10-11)
5 (Is. 39:7-8)   15 (Is. 7:1-2)
3 (Jer. 45)   20 (Jer. 11:21)
4 (Jer. 43:5-6)   18 (Jer. 46:2)
7 (Jer. 28:10-11)   12 (Jer. 39:9)
1 (Is. 8:6-7)   13 (Is. 7:1-2)
8 (Is. 37:36-37)   11 (Is. 36:1-2; 37:37)
2 (Is. 44:28)   14 (Jer. 43:5-6)
6 (Jer. 15:10-12, 17-18) 19 (Jer. 7:31)
9 (Jer. 27:8)   17 (Jer. 39:8;
                          Intro, p. 11)

Events (5)

1. c (Jer. 7:1-3, 4, 14, 24; 26:5-6, 9)
2. b (Jer. 11:21; 18:18; 19:10; 38:6)
3. a (Jer. 29:1-9)
4. d (Jer. 32:6-9; 37:11-14)
5. d (Jer. 36:4-6, 23)

C. PROPHECY (25)

Signs (15)

7 (Jer. 1:14)   11 (Jer. 17:7-8)
1 (Jer. 24)   15 (Lam. 1:1)
2 (Is. 20:3-5)   9 (Jer. 13:7-8)
4 (Is. 7:4-16)   10 (Jer. 17:5-6)
8 (Is. 11:1)   14 (Jer. 43:7-8)
5 (Jer. 1:11-12)   13 (Jer. 27:2-6)
6 (Is. 25:6-8)   12 (Jer. 18:6-10)
3 (Is. 9:6-7)

About Prophecies (10)

1. c (Is. 7:1-2;   6. b (Jer. 23:5-6)
   22:12-14; 28:1-7)   7. d (Jer. 5:19; 28:16-17;
2. d (Is. 9:2-4)   39:1-3)
3. a (Is. 11:11;   8. b (Is. 29:13; Jer. 13:15;
   41:27)   29:7)
4. c (Is. 53:8-10)   9. d (Is. 9:1-7)
5. a (Is. 61:1)   10. b (Is. 19:24)

D. FEATURES (30)

Background (9)   Special Content (8)
(See introductions)
                           1 (Is. 35:8)
1. destruction (or judgment) 1 (Is. 5:1-7)
2. poetry   2 (Is. 53)
3. the Messiah   1 (Is. 9:6)
4. returned, Jerusalem   2 (Is. 43:19)
5. spiritual life (or   J (Jer. 31:33)
   personal experiences)   J (Jer. 19)
6. doom   L (Lam. 1:1 and
7. changed   throughout)
8. sin
9. approval (or
   acceptance),
   judgment

Quotations (13)

2 (Is. 40:3)   3 (Is. 61:1)
J (Jer. 7:3)   J (Jer. 33:17)
1 (Is. 6:3)   1 (Is. 25:8)
2 (Is. 55:1)   2 (Is. 53:5)
L (Lam. 1:18)   L (Lam. 1:5)
J (Jer. 5:19)   1 (Is. 8:8)
                     2 (Is. 40:1)

PRE-TEST Unit 2 *(100 points)*

A. STRUCTURE *(16)*

Outline *(5)*	Sequence *(11)*	
	Ezekiel	Daniel
1. a		
2. d	4	4
3. b	5	2
4. b	1	5
5. c	3	3
	6	1
	2	

B. NARRATIVE *(14)*

Persons *(8)*		Events *(6)*
6	5	1. b
3	1	2. d
8	4	3. b
7	2	4. a
		5. c
		6. d

C. PROPHECY *(45)*

Signs *(20)*		Visions *(10)*
6	14	8
10	19	10
4	18	4
9	20	9
2	13	3
7	16	6
8	11	2
1	17	5
5	12	7
3	15	1

About Prophecies *(15)*

1. a	10	14
2. c	15	13
3. d	9	6
4. d	12	11
5. a	7	8

D. FEATURES *(25)*

Background *(12)*

E	D	D
D	D	E
E	E	E
D	E	E

Special Content *(13)*

E	E
D	D
D	E
E,D	D
D	D
E	E

SECTION TEST 1 – Ezekiel 1--24 *(33 points)*

A. STRUCTURE *(6)*

Outline *(3)*

1. Before, Fall, Jerusalem
2. Ezekiel's Call, First Vision
3. Doom, Jerusalem

Sequence *(3)*

3, 2, 1

C. PROPHECY *(20)*

Signs/Visions *(13)*		About Prophecies *(7)*
3	5	1. d
10	7	2. d
2	11	3. b
9	12	4. a
1	4	5. b
13	8	6. b
6		7. c

D. FEATURES *(7)*

Background *(3)*

1. Babylon or exile
2. Exiled, Jehoiachin
3. Jerusalem, Babylon

Special Content *(4)*

2
3
5
6

SECTION TEST 2 – Ezekiel 25--48 *(33 points)*

A. STRUCTURE *(10)*

Outline *(7)*

1. Judgment, Nations
2. Tyre, Palestinean Neighbors
3. Egypt
4. After, Fall, Jerusalem
5. Promise, Hope
6. Against Gog
7. Worshiping Community Restored

Sequence *(3)*

1, 3, 2

C. PROPHECY *(15)*

Signs/Visions *(6)*	About Prophecies *(9)*	
6	1. d	6. d
3	2. b	7. d
1	3. a	8. a
4	4. c	9. c
2	5. b	
5		

D. FEATURES *(8)*

Background *(3)*

1. Individual responsible
2. Fall of Jerusalem
3. Covenant

Special Content *(5)*

1, 3, 5, 8, 9

SECTION TEST 3 – Daniel *(50 points)*

A. STRUCTURE *(16)*

Outline *(12)*

I. Stories, Daniel, Friends
  1. Royal Food Refused
  2. Nebuchadnezzar's Dream
  3. Blazing Furnace
  4. Nebuchadnezzar's Madness
  5. Belshazzar's Banquet
  6. Daniel, Pit, Lions
II. Visions, Daniel
  7. Four Beasts
  8. Ram, Goat
  9. Seventy Years
  10. Angel, Tigris River

Sequence *(4)*

4
2
1
3

B. NARRATIVE *(12)*

Persons *(7)*	
2	6
1	5
4	7
3	

Events *(5)*

1. c
2. b
3. a
4. d
5. d

C. PROPHECY *(10)*

Signs *(6)*		Visions *(4)*
2	1	7
5	4	10
6	3	9
		8

D. FEATURES *(12)*

Background *(6)*		Special Content *(6)*	
1. Writings	4. Apocalyptic	1	8
2. Exile	5. Israel	2	10
3. Maccabees	6. History	6	11

UNIT TEST 2 *(100 points)*

A. STRUCTURE *(16)*

Outline *(5) (See page 60.)*

1. Before, Fall, Jerusalem
2. Judgment, Nations
3. After, Fall, Jerusalem
4. Stories, Daniel, Friends
5. Visions, Daniel

Sequence *(11)*

3 (Ez. 3:26)	5 (Dn. 5:29)
6 (Ez. 33:22)	4 (Dn. 4:31-34)
2 (Ez. 2:3)	2 (Dn. 2:48)
4 (Ez. 24:18)	1 (Dn. 1:3-6)
5 (Ez. 33:21)	3 (Dn. 3:16-21)
1 (Ez. 1:1)	

(Continued on next page)

B. NARRATIVE (14)

Persons (8)	Events (6)
8 (Ez. 38:2)	1. b (Ez. 1; 24; 5; 11)
5 (Dn. 1:7)	2. d (Dn. 2:7-13, 18)
1 (Ez. 1:1)	3. a (Dn. 3:18)
4 (Dn. 1:7)	4. c (Dn. 4:22; 4:16, 25, 26)
2 (Dn. 1:7)	5. d (Dn. 5:5, 24-28)
7 (Dn. 5:1)	6. d (Dn. 6:14, 16, 23)
3 (Dn. 1:7)	
6 (Dn. 1:8-11)	

C. PROPHECY (45)

Signs (20)

		Visions (10)
3 (Ez. 12)	17 (Ez. 34:11)	5 (Ez. 1:28)
9 (Ez. 24)	12 (Ez. 37:15-22)	9 (Ez. 48:35)
8 (Ez. 23)	19 (Ez. 33:8)	6 (Ez. 9:4)
2 (Ez. 5)	14 (Ez. 32:2)	2 (Ez. 10)
7 (Ez. 21)	11 (Dn. 2:19)	7 (Ez. 47:9)
1 (Ez. 4)	18 (Dn. 5:5, 26)	10 (Dn. 7:17-18)
10 (Ez. 24)	20 (Dn. 6:13-16)	8 (Dn. 12:1)
5 (Ez. 22)	13 (Dn. 1:13-15)	4 (Ez. 37)
4 (Ez. 13)	16 (Dn. 4:23-34)	1 (Dn. 9:24-25)
6 (Ez. 17)	15 (Dn. 3:18, 21)	3 (Dn. 8:3, 5, 25)

About Prophecies (15)

1. b (Ez. 8:3)	13 (Ez. 11:19-20)
2. a (Ez. 10:18-19)	15 (Ez. 18:2-4)
3. d (Ez. 17:13-20)	14 (Ez. 33:15)
4. d (Ez. 11:17; 40--43)	9 (Ez. 33:7-8)
5. c (Ez. 29:19, 21)	11 (Ez. 26:2-3)
6. a (Ez. 38:1-8)	10 (Ez. 32:21-32)
7. c (Ez. 43:2-4)	12 (Ez. 40:3, 6)
8. d (Ez. 47:12)	

D. FEATURES (25)

Background (13)	Special Content (12)
E (1:1-2)	E (1:3)
E (p. 61)	E (2:1) D (8:17)
D (p. 61)	D (3:29)
D (p. 61)	E (1:26)
E (11:16)	E (33:7)
D (p. 61)	D (5:23)
E (p. 61)	D (6:23)
D (p. 61)	D (8:16; 10:13)
E (5:7)	E (37:3)
E (11:17-20)	E (47:9)
E (18:20)	D (7:27)
D (p. 61)	D (9:26)
E (p. 61)	

ANSWERS TO TESTS IN UNIT 3

PRE-TEST Unit 3 (100 points)

A. STRUCTURE (12)

4	5	11
7	1	6
12	9	8
10	2	3

B. NARRATIVE (15)

Persons (9)		Places (6)	
6	5	2	3
9	4	6	1
3	1	4	5
2	7		
8			

C. PROPHECY (30)

Signs and Visions (18)				About Prophecies (12)		
7	4	14	18	1. a	5. d	9. d
3	6	13, 16	17	2. d	6. b	10. d
9	10	15	11	3. b	7. b	11. a
8	5	12		4. d	8. a	12. c
1	2					

D. FEATURES (43)

Background (19)	
1. marriage, living parable	8th
2. social justice	6th or 5th
3. exclusivism	7th
4. compassion (or love)	7th
5. Persian	8th
6. leaders	8th
7. rebuilding, Temple	7th
8. messianic age (coming Messiah)	6th
9. covenant renewal	6th
	5th

Special Content (24)

1. Jonah	9. Habakkuk	17. Malachi
2. Amos	10. Zephaniah	18. Joel
3. Zechariah	11. Hosea	19. Haggai
4. Hosea	12. Malachi	20. Joel
5. Zechariah	13. Joel	21. Micah
6. Hosea	14. Habakkuk	22. Joel
7. Nahum	15. Malachi	23. Amos
8. Micah	16. Amos	24. Hosea

SECTION TEST 1 (33 points)

A. STRUCTURE (6)

Outline (6)

1. Hosea's Marriage, Living Parable	3. Repentance, Promise
2. Israel's Crimes, Punishment	4. Plague, Locusts
	5. Promise, Restoration
	6. Day, Lord

C. PROPHECY (15)

Signs and Visions (8)		About Prophecies (7)	
6	1	1. c	5. c
7	8	2. a	6. a
2	4	3. a	7. a
5	3	4. b	

D. FEATURES (12)

Background (4)	Quotations (8)	
1. Marriage, love	1. H	5. J
2. Northern Kingdom, Samaria	2. J	6. H
3. Persian	3. J	7. H
4. plague, locusts, Day, Lord	4. H	8. J

SECTION TEST 2 (33 points)

A. STRUCTURE (9)

1. Judgment: Israel's Neighbors, Israel
2. Warnings, Israel
3. Five Visions
4. Punishment, Edom
5. Day, Lord
6. Jonah Disobeys, Lord
7. Jonah's Prayer
8. Jonah Obeys, Lord
9. Jonah's Anger, God's Mercy

C. PROPHECY (14)

3	5	10. a
8	9	11. d
4	2	12. c
6	1	13. d
	7	14. d

(Continued on next page)

D. FEATURES (10)

Background (5)	Special Content (5)
1. social justice	J
2. before, Northern	A
3. after	J
4. Assyrian	O
5. compassion (or love), all	A

SECTION TEST 3 (33 points)

A. STRUCTURE (10)

1. Messages, All Nations
2. Messages, Israel: Warning, Hope
3. Judgment, Nineveh
4. Fall, Nineveh
5. Habakkuk's Dialogue, God
6. Doom, Unrighteous
7. Habakkuk's Prayer
8. Day, Lord
9. Doom, Israel's Neighbors
10. Jerusalem's Doom, Redemption

C. PROPHECY (12)

8	5	9. d
3	4	10. a
6	2	11. c
7	1	12. d

D. FEATURES (11)

Background (5)

1. 8th
2. leaders (or capitals), judgment
3. public worship
4. 7th
5. idolatry

Special Content (6)

H	H
N	M
M	Z

SECTION TEST 4 (33 points)

A. STRUCTURE (6)

1. Rebuild, Temple
2. Promise, Zerubbabel
3. Prophecies, Time, Zerubbabel
4. Messiah, Future Deliverance
5. Israel's Sins
6. God's Judgment, Mercy

B. NARRATIVE (6)

3	2
1	4
5	1

C. PROPHECY (11)

Signs and Visions (7)	About Prophecies (4)
6　5	1. c
3　1,7	2. a
2　4	3. d
	4. d

D. FEATURES (10)

Background (5)	Special Content (5)
1. 520	Z
2. restoration (or rebuilding)	H
3. messianic	M
4. after	M
5. renewal, covenant	Z

UNIT TEST 3 (100 points)

A. STRUCTURE (31) (See outlines on page 96.)

1. Hosea's Marriage, Living Parable
2. Israel's Crimes, Punishment
3. Repentance, Promise
4. Plague, Locusts
5. Promise, Restoration
6. Day, Lord
7. Judgment: Israel's Neighbors, Israel
8. Warnings, Israel
9. Five Visions
10. Punishment, Edom
11. Day, Lord
12. Jonah Disobeys, Lord
13. Jonah's Prayer
14. Jonah Obeys, Lord
15. Jonah's Anger, God's Mercy
16. Messages, Nations
17. Messages, Israel: Warning, Hope
18. Judgment, Nineveh
19. Fall, Nineveh
20. Habakkuk's Dialogue, God
21. Doom, Unrighteous
22. Habakkuk's Prayer
23. Day, Lord
24. Doom, Israel's Neighbors
25. Jerusalem's Doom, Redemption
26. Rebuild, Temple
27. Promise, Zerubbabel
28. Prophecies, Time, Zerubbabel
29. Messiah, Future Deliverance
30. Israel's Sins
31. God's Judgment, Mercy

B. NARRATIVE (10)

6 (Zec. 4:8–10)
3 (Hg. 1:8)
4 (Nh. 1:15)
2 (Hg. 1:14)
1 (Am. 7:10)
5 (Am 7:9)
8 (Am. 3:14)
10 (Jon. 1:2, 3)
9 (Ob. 10–14)
7 (Am. 1:1)

C. PROPHECY (24)

Signs and Visions (12)	About Prophecies (12)
7 (Zec. 3:9)	1. b (Ho. 6:6)
3 (Ho. 1:2–3)	2. d (Jl. 2:32)
5 (Zec. 2:1–4)	3. a (Am. 3:2)
12 (Zec. 1:18–21)	4. d (Ob. 13–14)
11 (Zec. 4:11–14)	5. c (Jon. 3:4–10)
9 (Jl. 2:1–11)	6. d (Mic. 3:11)
2 (Ho. 7:11)	7. a (Nh. 1:11)
1 (Zec. 11:4–17)	8. d (Hb. 3:2; 2:4)
10 (Am. 7:1–6)	9. d (Zep. 3:8–9)
6 (Ho. 7:8–9)	10. c (Hg. 1:4–11)
8 (Ho. 1:2)	11. b (Zec. 4:6–7)
4 (Zec. 9:9)	12. a (Ml. 1:8; 3:2–3, 8–10)

D. FEATURES (35)

Background (15)
(See book introductions in guided reading for further information about answers.)

1. social justice (or judgment), Israel (or Northern Kingdom)			
2. Assyrian			
3. rebuilding	8th	8th	6th
4. visions, Messiah	6th or 5th	8th	5th
5. covenant renewal	7th	7th	
	7th	6th	

Special Content (20)

1. Jl. (3:10)	11. Zec. (9:9)
2. Jl. (2:1–11)	12. Zec. (11:12)
3. Am. (7:7; 8:1)	13. Nh. (1:15)
4. Hb. (1:1–4)	14. Zep. (2:3)
5. Ml. (4:5)	15. Ho. (11:1)
6. Hb. (2:20)	16. Jl. (2:28)
7. Mic. (6:8)	17. Ml. (3:1)
8. Ho. (11:8)	18. Ml. (4:2)
9. Am. (5:24)	19. Hg. (1:4)
10. Jon. (1:17)	20. Mic. (4:3)

SCORING TESTS

After checking answers for a test, record the number correct for each category in the blanks in # column. (To find % score for each category, follow directions, using % charts on pages 137-138 or by multiplying.) Then add the number correct in the categories to find the total correct for the test and follow directions for the % score. Record the test score here and on the growth record, page 138.

UNIT 1

Pre-test for Unit 1 *(100)*

Category	# Correct		% Score	Directions
A. Structure *(17)*	_____	=	_____	See % chart for 17.
B. Narrative *(30)*	_____	=	_____	See % chart for 30.
C. Prophecy *(25)*	_____	=	_____	# correct x 4.
D. Features *(28)*	_____	=	_____	See % chart for 28.
Total (A+B+C+D)	_____	=	_____	# correct is %.

Section Test 1 *(50)*

Category	# Correct		% Score	Directions
A. Structure *(10)*	_____	=	_____	# correct x 10.
B. Narrative *(13)*	_____	=	_____	See % chart for 13.
C. Prophecy *(12)*	_____	=	_____	See % chart for 12.
D. Features *(15)*	_____	=	_____	See % chart for 15.
Total (A+B+C+D)		=	_____	Multiply by 2.

Section Test 2 *(25)*

Category	# Correct		% Score	Directions
A. Structure *(4)*	_____	=	_____	# correct x 25.
B. Narrative *(8)*	_____	=	_____	See % chart for 8.
C. Prophecy *(5)*	_____	=	_____	# correct x 20.
D. Features *(8)*	_____	=	_____	See % chart for 8.
Total (A+B+C+D)		=	_____	Multiply by 4.

Section Test 3 *(20)*

Category	# Correct		% Score	Directions
A. Structure *(7)*	_____	=	_____	See % chart for 7.
C. Prophecy *(4)*	_____	=	_____	# correct x 25.
D. Features *(9)*	_____	=	_____	See % chart for 9.
Total (A+C+D)		=	_____	Multiply by 5.

Section Test 4 *(25)*

Category	# Correct		% Score	Directions
A. Structure *(5)*	_____	=	_____	# correct x 20.
B. Narrative *(5)*	_____	=	_____	# correct x 20.
C. Prophecy *(10)*	_____	=	_____	# correct x 10.
D. Features *(5)*	_____	=	_____	# correct x 20.
Total (A+B+C+D)		=	_____	Multiply by 4.

UNIT 1 *(continued)*

Section Test 5 *(50)*

Category	# Correct		% Score	Directions
A. Structure *(8)*	_____	=	_____	See % chart for 8.
B. Narrative *(19)*	_____	=	_____	See % chart for 19.
C. Prophecy *(11)*	_____	=	_____	See % chart for 11.
D. Features *(12)*	_____	=	_____	See % chart for 12.
Total (A+B+C+D)	_____	=	_____	Multiply by 2.

Unit Test 1 *(100)*

Category	# Correct		% Score	Directions
A. Structure *(20)*	_____	=	_____	# correct x 5.
B. Narrative *(25)*	_____	=	_____	# correct x 4.
C. Prophecy *(25)*	_____	=	_____	# correct x 4.
D. Features *(30)*	_____	=	_____	See % chart for 30.
Total (A+B+C+D)	_____	=	_____	# correct is %.

UNIT 2

Pre-test for Unit 2 *(100)*

Category	# Correct		% Score	Directions
A. Structure *(16)*	_____	=	_____	See % chart for 16.
B. Narrative *(14)*	_____	=	_____	See % chart for 14.
C. Prophecy *(45)*	_____	=	_____	See % chart for 45.
D. Features *(25)*	_____	=	_____	# correct x 4.
Total (A+B+C+D)	_____	=	_____	# correct is %.

Section Test 1 *(33)*

Category	# Correct		% Score	Directions
A. Structure *(6)*	_____	=	_____	See % chart for 6.
C. Prophecy *(20)*	_____	=	_____	# correct x 5.
D. Features *(7)*	_____	=	_____	See % chart for 7.
Total (A+C+D)	_____	=	_____	Multiply by 3; then add 1.

Section Test 2 *(33)*

Category	# Correct		% Score	Directions
A. Structure *(10)*	_____	=	_____	# correct x 10.
C. Prophecy *(15)*	_____	=	_____	See % chart for 15.
D. Features *(8)*	_____	=	_____	See % chart for 8.
Total (A+C+D)	_____	=	_____	Multiply by 3; then add 1.

UNIT 2 *(continued)*

Section Test 3 *(50)*

Category	# Correct	% Score	Directions
A. Structure *(16)*	_____ =	_____	See % chart for 16.
B. Narrative *(12)*	_____ =	_____	See % chart for 12.
C. Prophecy *(10)*	_____ =	_____	# correct x 10.
D. Features *(12)*	_____ =	_____	See % chart for 12.
Total (A+B+C+D)	=	_____	Multiply by 2.

Unit Test 2 *(100)*

Category	# Correct	% Score	Directions
A. Structure *(16)*	_____ =	_____	See % chart for 16.
B. Narrative *(14)*	_____ =	_____	See % chart for 14.
C. Prophecy *(45)*	_____ =	_____	See % chart for 45.
D. Features *(25)*	_____ =	_____	# correct x 4.
Total (A+B+C+D)	=	_____	# correct is %.

UNIT 3

Pre-test for Unit 3 *(100)*

Category	# Correct	% Score	Directions
A. Structure *(12)*	_____ =	_____	See % chart for 12.
B. Narrative *(15)*	_____ =	_____	See % chart for 15.
C. Prophecy *(30)*	_____ =	_____	See % chart for 30.
D. Features *(43)*	_____ =	_____	See % chart for 43.
Total (A+B+C+D)	=	_____	# correct is %.

Section Test 1 *(33)*

Category	# Correct	% Score	Directions
A. Structure *(6)*	_____ =	_____	See % chart for 6.
C. Prophecy *(15)*	_____ =	_____	See % chart for 15.
D. Features *(12)*	_____ =	_____	See % chart for 12.
Total (A+C+D)	=	_____	Multiply by 3; then add 1.

UNIT 3 *(continued)*

Section Test 2 *(33)*

Category	# Correct	% Score	Directions
A. Structure *(9)*	_____ =	_____	See % chart for 9.
C. Prophecy *(14)*	_____ =	_____	See % chart for 14.
D. Features *(10)*	_____ =	_____	# correct x 10.
Total (A+C+D)	=	_____	Multiply by 3; then add 1.

Section Test 3 *(33)*

Category	# Correct	% Score	Directions
A. Structure *(10)*	_____ =	_____	# correct x 10.
C. Prophecy *(12)*	_____ =	_____	See % chart for 12.
D. Features *(11)*	_____ =	_____	See % chart for 11.
Total (A+C+D)	=	_____	Multiply by 3; then add 1.

Section Test 4 *(33)*

Category	# Correct	% Score	Directions
A. Structure *(6)*	_____ =	_____	See % chart for 6.
B. Narrative *(6)*	_____ =	_____	See % chart for 6.
C. Prophecy *(11)*	_____ =	_____	See % chart for 11.
D. Features *(10)*	_____ =	_____	# correct x 10.
Total (A+B+C+D)	=	_____	Multiply by 3; then add 1.

Unit Test 3 *(100)*

Category	# Correct	% Score	Directions
A. Structure *(31)*	_____ =	_____	See % chart for 31.
B. Narrative *(10)*	_____ =	_____	# correct x 10.
C. Prophecy *(24)*	_____ =	_____	See % chart for 24.
D. Features *(35)*	_____ =	_____	See % chart for 35.
Total (A+B+C+D)	=	_____	# correct is %.

% CHARTS FOR SCORING

6#	1	2	3	4	5	6	#
%	17	33	50	67	83	100	%

7#	1	2	3	4	5	6	7	#
%	14	29	43	57	71	86	100	%

8#	1	2	3	4	5	6	7	8	#
%	13	25	38	50	63	75	86	100	%

9#	1	2	3	4	5	6	7	8	9	#
%	11	22	33	44	56	67	78	89	100	%

11#	1	2	3	4	5	6	7	8	9	10	11	#
%	9	18	27	36	45	55	64	73	82	91	100	%

12#	1	2	3	4	5	6	7	8	9	10	11	12	#
%	9	17	25	34	42	50	59	67	75	84	92	100	%

13#	1	2	3	4	5	6	7	8	9	10	11	12	13	#
%	8	16	23	31	38	46	54	62	69	77	85	92	100	%

14#	1	2	3	4	5	6	7	8	9	10	11	12	13	14	#
%	7	14	21	28	36	43	50	57	64	72	79	86	93	100	%

15#	1	2	3	4	5	6	7	8	9	10	11	12	13	14	15	#
%	7	13	20	27	33	40	47	53	60	67	73	80	87	93	100	%

16#	1	2	3	4	5	6	7	8	9	10	11	12	13	14	15	16	#
%	7	13	19	25	31	37	44	50	56	63	69	75	81	87	94	100	%

17#	1	2	3	4	5	6	7	8	9	10	11	12	13	14	15	16
%	6	12	17	23	29	35	41	47	53	58	64	70	76	82	88	94

#	17	%
%	100	%

19#	1	2	3	4	5	6	7	8	9	10	11	12	13	14	15	16
%	5	10	15	21	26	31	37	42	47	53	58	63	69	74	79	85

#	17	18	19	#
%	90	95	100	%

24#	1	2	3	4	5	6	7	8	9	10	11	12	13	14	15	16
%	4	8	13	17	21	25	29	33	37	42	46	50	54	58	63	67

#	17	18	19	20	21	22	23	24	#
%	71	75	79	83	88	92	96	100	%

28#	1	2	3	4	5	6	7	8	9	10	11	12	13	14	15	16
%	4	8	11	14	18	21	25	28	32	36	39	43	46	50	54	57

#	17	18	19	20	21	22	23	24	25	26	27	28	#
%	61	64	68	71	75	79	82	86	89	93	96	100	%

30#	1	2	3	4	5	6	7	8	9	10	11	12	13	14	15	16
%	3	7	10	13	17	20	23	27	30	33	37	40	43	47	50	53

#	17	18	19	20	21	22	23	24	25	26	27	28	29	30	#
%	57	60	63	67	70	73	76	80	83	87	90	93	97	100	%

31#	1	2	3	4	5	6	7	8	9	10	11	12	13	14	15	16
%	3	6	10	13	16	19	22	26	29	32	35	39	42	45	48	52

#	17	18	19	20	21	22	23	24	25	26	27	28	29	30	31	#
%	55	58	61	64	68	71	74	77	81	84	87	90	93	97	100	%

35#	1	2	3	4	5	6	7	8	9	10	11	12	13	14	15	16
%	3	6	9	11	14	17	20	23	26	29	31	34	37	40	43	46

#	17	18	19	20	21	22	23	24	25	26	27	28	29	30	31	32
%	49	51	54	57	60	63	66	69	71	74	77	80	83	86	89	91

#	33	34	35	#
%	94	97	100	%

43#	1	2	3	4	5	6	7	8	9	10	11	12	13	14	15	16
%	2	5	7	9	12	14	16	18	20	23	25	27	30	32	35	37

#	17	18	19	20	21	22	23	24	25	26	27	28	29	30	31	32
%	39	41	43	46	48	51	53	55	58	60	62	65	67	70	72	74

#	33	34	35	36	37	38	39	40	41	42	43	#
%	77	79	81	83	86	88	90	93	95	98	100	%

45#	1	2	3	4	5	6	7	8	9	10	11	12	13	14	15	16
%	2	4	7	9	11	13	15	18	20	22	24	26	29	31	33	36

#	17	18	19	20	21	22	23	24	25	26	27	28	29	30	31	32
%	38	40	42	44	46	48	51	53	56	58	60	62	64	67	69	71

#	33	34	35	36	37	38	39	40	41	42	43	44	45	#
%	73	76	78	80	82	84	87	89	91	93	96	98	100	%

BOOK FOUR GROWTH RECORD

To measure growth, subtract pre-test score from unit test score; enter difference in the growth column. (NOTE: Section test scores show progress along the way, but are not used in computing growth.)

UNIT 1: ISAIAH, JEREMIAH, AND LAMENTATIONS

Category	Pre-test	Section 1	Section 2	Section 3	Section 4	Section 5	Unit 1	Growth
A. Structure	%	%	%	%	%	%	%	%
B. Narrative	%	%	%		%	%	%	%
C. Prophecy	%	%	%	%	%	%	%	%
D. Features	%	%	%	%	%	%	%	%
Total	%	%	%	%	%	%	%	%

UNIT 2: EZEKIEL AND DANIEL

Category	Pre-test	Section 1	Section 2	Section 3	Unit 2	Growth
A. Structure	%	%	%	%	%	%
B. Narrative	%			%	%	%
C. Prophecy	%	%	%	%	%	%
D. Features	%	%	%	%	%	%
Total	%	%	%	%	%	%

UNIT 3: THE TWELVE

Category	Pre-test	Section 1	Section 2	Section 3	Section 4	Unit 3	Growth
A. Structure	%	%	%	%	%	%	%
B. Narrative	%				%	%	%
C. Prophecy	%	%	%	%	%	%	%
D. Features	%	%	%	%	%	%	%
Total	%	%	%	%	%	%	%